YOUR FIRST STEP IN HEAVEN

WHAT HAPPENS IMMEDIATELY AFTER DEATH

Wallace Henley

Your First Step in Heaven
Copyright © 2014 Wallace Henley

All rights reserved. No part of this publication may be reproduced, stored in a retrieval system, or transmitted in any form or by any means—electronic, mechanical, photocopying, recording, or otherwise—without the prior written permission of the publisher and copyright owners.

Cover art used by permission of iStock.com

Printed in the United States of America.

Unless otherwise noted all Scripture quotations are taken from the NEW AMERICAN STANDARD BIBLE © The Lockman Foundation.

EBook: 978-1-312-07911-3
Softcover: 978-1-312-62320-0
Hardcover: 978-1-312-07909-0

TABLE OF CONTENTS

INTRODUCTION Up the Mountain Into Light..................................7

PART 1 PROLOGUE: BO'S PASSAGE 13

Chapter 1 Peace and Joy on a Talladega hillside 15

Chapter 2 Being is better than existence...37

PART 2 YOUR PASSAGE..55

Chapter 3 Where Is Heaven? 57

Chapter 4 Stepping Out, Stepping In The New Body 79

Chapter 5 Stepping Out, Stepping In..99

Chapter 6 Standing Before the Seven Eyes 121

Chapter 7 Whom will you know? 135

Chapter 8 What about those you won't see?.................................. 147

Chapter 9 Will We See Loved Ones Who Never Heard the Gospel?............. 159

Chapter 10 On Your First Step in Heaven You Will Enter Your Special Place175

INTRODUCTION
Up the Mountain Into Light

I am enjoying getting old. I recommend it for everyone.

Some people see aging as a slow decline into a deep dark valley where there are lots of woeful things lurking in the shadows. As I write I am in my 70s, and have noticed some changes. After more than a decade of jogging almost daily my ankles fuss at me. Driving at night is a beautiful experience because the cataracts in my eyes turn light beams into spears of glorious color emitting a lavish spray into the darkness. I get to watch my favorite old movies a lot because I have never seen the end of many of them since I fall asleep before they're over. ("Honey," my wife said awhile back, "do you know they make movies in color now?")

Despite those tints of aging, I have never been more excited in my passage through this world that began in 1941. I don't see getting old as a descent into a chasm. Rather, *aging is an ascent up the mountain into the light.*

I've climbed a few mountains in my life, but the most unforgettable was a seven-hour ride on horseback to the peak of a Colorado Rocky. Down at the base it was a pleasant June day near Buena Vista. Leon—one of my best buddies who happens also to be my brother-in-law—and I drove up to the ghost town of St. Elmo, Colorado, where we met our guide and fellow wranglers. We spent the first couple of hours on a pleasant jaunt through lush high meadows. As we approached the base of the mountain we could see snow way up top above the tree-line. As a fellow from south Texas the blanket of white stirred my anticipation.

The snow up top was deeper than our guide realized. We rounded the summit, and began the trek downward, but lost the path in the snow banks. Staring down and trying to guide my horse's steps, I noted a miracle: my eyes saw clearer than ever. That's because way up high, the light is much brighter. It seemed I could see everything better from high on that Colorado peak. I could look back down the mountain and see where we had been, and just beyond the summit I could see the promising area where we were headed just over the top where the snow had melted and footing would be more secure.

I learned a couple of important lessons on that ride years ago that transformed my way of thinking about aging and death.

The view from the mountain

First, the higher you go up the mountain of time, the more you can see the trail that got you up the slopes, and the meaning of it. Just yesterday from this moment of writing, Irene and I attended the funeral for her mother, who died just shy of 95. On our visits with her in the last years of her life we could tell that she could see where she had been in life. Experiences that had once brought pain were transformed through her lofty perspective into vital components of her life journey that had ultimately brought joy and blessing. Even now, though I am "only" in my 70s, I can look back on mistakes I made, and see how God used them to bring me into the destiny He had for me. From up here on the mount of aging you can see that "all things" really do "work together for good to those who love God and are called to His purposes!" (Romans 8:28)

I think of what Moses' view must have been like up on Mount Nebo, as he was about to die. The Hebrew wanderers were down there at the base of the mountain, readying to cross into the Promised Land under the command of Joshua, his successor. Moses could look back up the trail that got Israel to that pivotal point and him up on Nebo. Though he could not enter, the Lord let him see where his people were headed—and he no doubt sensed he was going to an even better place. The past ordeal in the wilderness added up to destiny, and Moses had the joy of seeing the whole panorama.

Maybe he winced as he remembered the moment he struck the rock from anger. But in the light at the top of the mountain perhaps Moses could also see the grace of God covering his error back there on the road of time, and knew God's great peace available on the summit for people who, in the words of Proverbs 3:5-6, trust the Lord with all their hearts, refuse to lean on their own understanding, and in all their ways acknowledge Him.

'A strong reassurance of ultimate peace'

Such folk turned one of the modern world's most famous scientists to Christ. Dr. Frank Collins, MD, and perhaps the world's top geneticist—he was picked to lead the successful mission to read the human genome—started his career as an avowed atheist. In his third year of medical school, as a young intern in a North Carolina hospital, Collins entered into "intense experiences involving the care of patients." As he dealt with seriously ill people, the "taboos that normally prevent the exchange of intensely private information (came) tumbling down along with the sensitive physical contract between the ill person and the healer." Collins fought had to "maintain the professional distance and lack of emotional involvement that many of my teachers advocated."

Ultimately, Collins was impacted powerfully by the witness of some of his patients. "What struck me profoundly about my bedside conversations with these good North Carolina people was the spiritual aspect of what many of them were going through." Many were strong believers in the God Collins did not believe existed. But, he wrote years later, "I witnessed numerous cases of individuals whose faith provided them a strong reassurance of ultimate peace, be it in this world or the next."

Once, while working with an elderly patient suffering severe heart pain, Collins faced what he described as his "most awkward moment." She wanted to know what her young doctor believed about life and death. "I felt my face flush as I stammered out the words, 'I'm not really sure,'" Collins replied. The woman's question spurred him to deeper consideration of the possibility of God's existence, a process that would lead Collins not only to belief in God but to serious commitment to Christ.[1]

Patients like her had that "strong reassurance of ultimate peace" not only because of the perspective that helped them make greater sense of God's work in their past, but because they were *high enough up to begin to get a glimpse of where they were going.*

No one saw it better than Jesus that day at Caesarea Philippi when Peter challenged His decision to go to Jerusalem where He would be in danger of arrest and execution. "Get behind me, Satan!" Jesus replied to Peter, doubtless stunning him. Peter could only see the danger, but Jesus could see "over the mountain." He knew the cross stood at its peak, but also that there was an open tomb beyond.

Suffering gets us high up the mountain fast. Jesus was only 33 when He moved forward in the assurance of eternity. I have also seen young cancer patients who got the glimpse of Heaven beyond the summit of time and who went forward with immense peace. I think of one in particular, a 23-year old mother, who appeared to be dying with the malignancy. There was a point at which her text messages and verbal communications to me turned to the

---

[1] Collins tells his story in his powerful book, *The Language of God,* New York: Simon & Schuster/Free Press.

theme of peace and joy, *no matter what*. Though young, her ordeal had rocketed her up the mountain. As I write, she is in remission and going strong, but has peace and joy whatever the outcome.

The big 'if'

These realities are contingent on a big factor: They are possible in their full scope only as we age or suffer in Christ. What does that mean?
- His grace in the past.
- His hope in the present.
- His peace and joy about the future.

In more than four decades as a pastor I have walked with many people through their dying-times, and been with a lot of them when they crossed into eternity. Hardly any are as dear in my memory as that of Pastor Bo Adkison, beloved friend and colleague at a church I served as senior pastor. To set the stage for considering *your* passage (and mine) we'll first look at "Bo's Passage." Then we'll look in some detail at your first step in Heaven.

I pray what you read in Bo's story and the subsequent chapters will be used of God to give you, like the people Francis Collins observed long ago, "strong reassurance of ultimate peace, be it in this world or the next," regarding your own passage, and that of your loved ones.

PART 1
PROLOGUE: BO'S PASSAGE

Chapter 1

PEACE AND JOY ON A TALLADEGA HILLSIDE

There is a breeze-swathed hillside overlooking the quaint, history-wizened buildings of Talladega, Alabama, that is holy ground to me. It bears the graves of my grandmother, the grandfather I remember seeing only once, in early 1945, my father, and aunts and uncles.

The first time I was there was 1956, when I was 15 years old. The occasion was the burial of my grandmother, my father's mom. Daddy would be buried there in exactly a decade, followed a few years later by aunts and uncles.

Scattered here and there in the old pre-Civil War cemetery are the graves of others of my relatives. It was these folk and their neighbors who gave the early definition to "Talladega Nights." The booming raceway over the hills to the north, near I-20, wasn't even the wisp of a thought when my kin hunted, fished, played, courted, married and established homes and families in the pine-forested hills and valleys of Talladega County.

But the grave that I linger over the most is that of my dad, who was born in 1907 and died in 1966. Somewhere in the crunch of gritty poverty, backwoods brew, grim prospects, Depression-era despair, coupled with an overwhelming passion to break free and succeed in life, delusion rooted in his mind. By the time I came along in 1941, dad was already bumping into walls every time he tried to hurdle his crude beginnings. By 1945, to escape the frustration of what he perceived as failure, daddy began crawling more and more frequently into a big cave called "alcohol." Ultimately, it consumed him, and in 1966, at 59, he died of a bolting heart attack in a hospital while I stood at his side.

I am now an old man, having lived in this world much longer than my father did. Still, though, when I go to his grave every couple of years from my Texas home, I think about that dying moment I observed so long ago, and, strangely, am bathed in peace.

Despite his alcoholism and mental anguish, my father loved God passionately. Though he didn't finish high school, he once wrote a booklet warning readers of the dangers of drinking. He earnestly wanted me to be a preacher, and few things made him happier than seeing me in the pulpit. I have no doubt he is Heaven, in the presence of the Lord. Dad's mind is clear, his emotions at peace, and the winsome personality cloaked by the alcohol now on full, delightful display.

That's why I experience peace and joy when I stand at his plot on that Talladega hillside.

But there have been lingering questions. His death was so sudden there was no warning, no opportunity to talk, no chance for him to describe his passage. What was it like at that quick fragment of a second when he was passing from this dimension into the Kingdom of Heaven? Was there a flash of time when part of him was in this world and another facet of his being already in Heaven? What did he experience in that passage?

After forays into politics and journalism, I became a pastor, seven years after my dad's passing. Over more than three decades, I have now observed death dozens of times. The questions I tossed around in my mind about my father's death-passage roll around again every time I watch people die. I seek answers as I attempt to help grieving loved ones work their way through their own passage of loss.

Biology and physiology can tell us all about what occurs to the body and its functions as a person dies. But what about the mind and emotions? Is there mental awareness during the death-passage? Do we experience anything emotionally as we slip away? Where does the human spirit go as we are crossing over? At what point does it leave the body?

The actual process of dying is a profound mystery. "I am about to take my last voyage, a great leap in the dark," cried the philosopher Thomas Hobbes, as he lay dying in 1679. Three centuries later, in 1941, the Irish writer, James Joyce, would face the mysterious passage, and ask, "Does nobody understand?"

Bo's Passage

There was one death-passage I observed in almost 40 years as a pastor that helped me at least begin to get answers to my questions. Bo Adkison was not a blood relative, but he may as well have been. We worked together for a decade. "Brother Bo" was the beloved associate pastor of the church where I was senior pastor.

Bo was the model pastor, and the people of our church loved and admired him, as I did. He was always perfectly groomed, professionally dressed and rarely took off his coat, even at the office. Bo was the picture of excellence, but also looked and acted like everyone's grandpa. When he visited sick folk at the hospital, he didn't keep glancing at his watch and intone a hurried, formula-style prayer. "Who's taking care of your cat?" he might ask the bedridden. "Can I get your clothes to the laundry?"

We coined his East Texas drawl and the expressions that rode along as "Bo-isms." They were priceless, and so was he.

One of my favorite memories of Bo was seeded during a staff retreat at a ranch on the edge of the Texas Hill Country. Our team had spent an extended time in worship and prayer. Quietness had settled across the gentle, rolling Texas prairies surrounding the ranch. The living room in the 100-year old house where we met was serene as a sanctuary.

Suddenly a shout shot from Bo that shook us all like a barrage of thunder after a lightning strike. At first we thought something was wrong, but then we heard Bo shouting over and over again, "Hallelujah… Hallelujah… Hallelujah!" Bo had experienced a "Holy Ghost" visitation in a direct, life-changing incursion straight into his heart.

In that moment, the Lord had revealed to Bo the nature of his ministry for the rest of his life. The vision of his destiny connected so completely with Bo's gifts, talents, skills, heart-desires and passions that everything had come suddenly into perfect alignment. Every experience of his past, all the hurts and pains, joys and successes became a symphony of meaning rather than a cacophony of unanswered questions.

I will always be grateful to God that I got to share that experience with Bo. It was genuinely extraordinary.

"What happened?" I asked, when Bo's tears of joy eased enough he could talk.

"*Gates to Splendor*," he replied.

When Bo regained his composure he explained that, while in prayer, God showed him that he was to have a special ministry to dying people, those, as he put it, in the "death channel." Specifically, Bo was to give the dying comfort and encouragement that death for the person secure in Christ, was a journey toward the "Gates" that opened to the glory and wonder of God. It is a passage not to be dreaded, but to be anticipated, not a dismal slide into darkness and hopelessness, but in Christ a wonderful, thrilling flight into peace and joy indescribable.

That's what made Bo shout.

In the ensuing years, I watched Bo carry out this ministry to others. He was a great blessing to the dying and their families.

And then it came time for Bo to enter the death channel. I had left the church where we served together three or four years earlier, and our contacts had been limited. Then someone told me Bo had been diagnosed with an aggressive cancer. I wanted to comfort this man I loved so much, but I also desired to see if Bo would feel the same way about the "death channel" that had made him shout that day perhaps a decade earlier. So, I visited him in the early stage at the hospital and later at home, as he lay on his death-bed.

The visits as he neared the "Gates to Splendor" were remarkable. Bo's mind was clear as a pristine brook. He reported what he was "seeing" in his inner man. I don't trust most "Near Death Experiences" (NDEs) as authoritative for a couple of reasons. First, they are intensely subjective. Trustworthy authority, on the other hand, is objective in its reality. It's not based on human perceptions, emotional experiences, or even mental reasoning. Second, it's possible that some NDEs are induced by medications given in the later stages of the death passage, or by reduction of oxygen to the brain.

However, Bo's passage was different. First, he was not comatose or in a drugged state when he described what he was seeing as he lay dying. He was nearing death, but not unconscious or in a hallucinatory state (I have seen such conditions many times over four decades). Second, Bo's was not an NDE, in which he "died" and "returned" to his body. Third, everything Bo reported was corroborated by the objective standard of Scripture.

We can trust NDEs—though, again, Bo's state was not that—when the experience of the apparently resuscitated person aligns with biblical revelation.

Verifying experiences

There are many tools and resources for corroborating a physical or natural phenomenon, but how can we verify experiences of the human soul and spirit? The instrument of corroboration must be *uniquely* qualified to address the specific claims or manifestations of given phenomena.

If the Bible is the revelation of the reality of a dimension that transcends the time-space-matter (natural) domain, and if death is a passage from the natural dimension into one that transcends, goes beyond, or is outside the natural (therefore transnatural), and if the Bible is revealed by the Intellect, or Mind underlying the transnatural dimension, then the Bible is the corroborating source for all interactions with the transnatural dimension, including interactions within the death passage.

This is not a study of apologetics, therefore I will not rally all the presuppositional and evidentiary evidences of the Bible's authenticity. Rather, I will rely on the fact of the existence of the centuries of study and the vast body of work that support the Bible as the Word of God.

But I will go beyond that. Mature faith recognizes that it is not the "evidences" that confirm the Bible, but the Bible that confirms the "evidences." *Thus, the fundamental presupposition of this study is that the Bible is the revelation of the nature and truth behind the transnatural dimension, and therefore the corroborating source for all claims relating to that realm, including those about human death.*

Bo described to me four different phenomena he was observing as he approached death: a City out on the horizon, the glory of God, especially His absolute purity, and Heaven's utter abhorrence of evil and the sin that is its expression. His demeanor and composure throughout the process, especially in light of his shock over sin, spoke eloquently about the immensity of God's grace.

Bo was lucid and calm when he discussed these observations, like a scientist reporting on the findings of an experimental project. Bo was comfortable, and eager to move forward in the journey.[2]

Three times in the Bible we have accounts of the dying process on the microcosmic scale of individuals. Two of them have to do with people who followed God transitioning to Heaven, and a surprising example shows graphically the horror of the individual passing into death without God.

The example of Enoch

Way back in time's early morning a godly man named Enoch had a dying experience that gives hope for

---

[2] The descriptions throughout this study of godly people in their death passages should not infer that they are always calm and unafraid. Oxygen deprivation, intense pain and trauma can sometimes cause the body to react in panic. If you observe a loved one in distress as he or she nears the death passage, it doesn't mean the person is separated from God, abandoned by Him or faithless. What is described in this book refers primarily to what happens to people after they have lost consciousness, and have actually entered the death passage.

everyone in true relationship with God. *The Amplified Bible* translates it like this:

> So all the days of Enoch were 365 years. And Enoch walked [in habitual fellowship] with God; and he was not, for God took him [home with Him]. (Genesis 5:23-24 AMP)

The Bible refers often to a person's "walk with God." For example, Romans 6:4 says, "as Christ was raised from the dead through the glory of the Father, so we too might walk in newness of life." Paul writes that the man and woman of God walk "by faith, not by sight" (2 Corinthians 5:7). He also encourages us to "walk by the spirit" so we won't "carry out the desire of the flesh."

To walk with God, then, is to maintain a closeness of relationship with Him that impacts and sets the standard for our behavior and work.

What Enoch's passage tells us is that the walk with God is a continuum. The person who was walked with God in the natural dimension, is, in a sense, already walking with Him in the transnatural realm. Therefore, the death passage for a man or woman in fellowship with God is simply a continuation of the "walk" on which they've already embarked.

Jesus said that in His Father's "house" are many "dwelling places" (John 14:2). We enter His "house" when we come into relationship with God through Jesus Christ. That happens in the world of space, time, and matter.

Therefore, dying is simply moving from one "dwelling place"—or room—in that great house to another!

The example of Elijah

The second experience reported in the Bible that helps provide a model for the dying process is that of Elijah. The Bible tells us that as Elijah and his protégé, Elisha, walked along they were talking, when suddenly,

> "a chariot of fire and horses of fire parted the two of them, and Elijah went up by a whirlwind into heaven. And Elisha saw it and he cried, My father, my father! The chariot of Israel and its horsemen! And he saw him no more. And he took hold of his own clothes and tore them in two pieces." (2 Kings 2:11-12 AMP)

There are several important insights about the dying process that we discover in Elijah's experience. First, the chariots and horses of fire are probably an angelic manifestation, as would be indicated by Ezekiel's vision:

> As I looked, behold, a storm wind was coming from the north, a great cloud with fire flashing forth continually and a bright light around it, and in its midst something like glowing metal in the midst of the fire. Within it there were

> figures resembling four living beings. And this was their appearance: they had human form. (Ezekiel 1:4-5 NASU)

Apparently, as Elisha watches Elijah's passage from this dimension, he is observing the manifestation of an angelic presence accompanying Elijah as he goes into the presence of God.

This is also the witness of Psalm 104:4 and Hebrews 1:7,

> Referring to the angels He says, [God] Who makes His angels winds and His ministering servants flames of fire... (AMP, quoting Psalm 104:4)

The "angel of death" is to those who die without God a terrifying reality, just as Christ as Lord is a frightening prospect to those who have rejected Him. However, Jesus Christ as Lord is a wonderful truth to those who know Him, and so angels are glorious companions to Christ-redeemed people in the death passage. They are, as Hebrews 1:14 puts it, "ministering spirits" to human beings who receive Christ's salvation.

Jesus Himself, in a parable, refers to angels as the "vehicle" by which human beings are transported from this world into the spiritual. "Now the poor man died and *was carried away by the angels* to Abraham's bosom," says Jesus, in telling the parable. (Luke 16:22, emphasis added)

The angels, Psalm 91:11 reveals, "guard" God's people "in all your ways." The root word for "guard" means "to exercise great care over."[3] Dying is an intricate passage, and the inference is that the angels watch over the individual making the journey.

When a man or woman is in the death passage, he or she is surrounded by angels. They are the "reapers" who "gather" people into the transnatural dimension. For the person going into absolute separation from God for eternity, the angels are "grim reapers," but for those inheriting Heaven, the angels are joyful "gatherers," delighting over the "harvesting" of the redeemed.

The second insight we can glean about the passage from this world into the heavenly dimension is that it is a "departure." Elijah goes from one place to another, as Elisha watches. This is also Paul's insight, as he writes, in 2 Timothy 4:6,

> "For I am already being poured out as a drink offering, and *the time of my departure* has come." (Emphasis added)

The assumption of the materialistic worldview is that dying has only to do with the body, and that death is annihilation. But the human being is also comprised of spirit and soul, and these components of the person go *somewhere*. In fact, the dying process is all about the movement of the

---

[3] *Theological Wordbook of the Old Testament.* Copyright (c) 1980 by The Moody Bible Institute of Chicago.

spirit and soul of the individual from one sphere into another.

Normally, we think of departures from our loved ones a sad thing. However, the person who dies in the Lord doesn't experience separation from those they cherish in the natural world. Time, in the spiritual dimension, has a different measure. To those who die in Christ, dying is like a person walking into another room, only to turn and see his or her loved ones have followed immediately.

Note also that Elijah went "up" into "heaven." "Up" is a relative term. From the perspective of the United States, "up," in Australia is "down," and vice-versa. For a person in Hawaii, "up," to an individual on a Caribbean isle might be "horizontal." Dying is stepping from the material dimension into the spiritual, which might be next to us. However, the heavenly dimension is "up" in a qualitative sense, in that it is a "better world" for those restored to relationship with God through Jesus Christ.

Paul wrote to the Philippians that, as he contemplated death, he was "hard-pressed from both directions, having the desire to depart and be with Christ, for that is very much better…" (Philippians 1:23) Further, the men and women of heroic faith, as shown by the Old Testament examples, "desire a better country, that is, a heavenly one," according to Hebrews 11:16.

When Irene and I first married, we lived in a tiny garage apartment. After a few months, we moved to a rickety old house that had been the 1930s-era parsonage for a church I served during college. I remember those places with happiness, and yet I would not go back to them, because Irene and I have made the passage to a "better place."

I remember our joyful anticipation every time we moved, the excitement of living in a nicer home. Each time we moved, along with the hard work, there was delight as we thought about where we were going. So it is for the person who dies in Christ. It is a passage of eager anticipation because it is movement to a "better place." In that sense, it is "upward," superior.

A final insight into the passage we discover from Elijah's experience is that it was glorious. Elisha is awestruck. "Elisha saw it and cried out, 'My father! My father! The chariots and charioteers of Israel!'" (2 Kings 2:12 NLT)

Twice in recent years I have seen people in awe over the death passage, even in the midst of their grief over the departure of their loved ones. In one case, a man described in wonder how he could actually see death moving over the body of his loved one. But she was safe in Christ, and he could look only with amazement as he watched death envelope her. It was as if she was being slowly immersed in a warm spring, with part of her body in the soothing waters, and the upper portion still on the "surface."

I was present decades ago with another man as his wife made the passage. He and his children and other immediate family surrounded the woman's bed. The whole family had a deep relationship with Christ, and the room was full of an atmosphere of quiet worship. As the young woman passed from the time-space-matter dimension into Heaven, there were tears mixed with grief and wonder. The presence of the Holy Spirit was tangible. Everyone knew they had observed, not shame and ignominy, but beauty. As I reflected on the lady's passage, I was reminded of the words of the Psalmist:

> How lovely are Your dwelling places, O LORD of hosts!
> My soul longed and even yearned for the courts of the LORD;
> My heart and my flesh sing for joy to the living God.
> The bird also has found a house,
> And the swallow a nest for herself, where she may lay her young,
> Even Your altars, O LORD of hosts,
> My King and my God.
> (Psalm 84:1-3 NASU)

The beauty experienced by those in covenant with God as they pass—and often by those who observe—helps us understand better the words in Psalm 116:15, "Precious in the sight of the LORD Is the death of His godly ones."

Technically, it could be argued that what Enoch and Elijah experienced was not the dying process, since they did not "see death." But what happened to both was a passage from one dimension, the natural, into another, the transnatural. Since this is the very essence of the dying process, the experience of the two men provides insights into the passage of every man and woman in relationship with God.

In fact, Enoch and Elijah reveal God's intentional will. The Father desires that we all move from earth to Heaven without death. But the fall had profound implications for the natural sphere. Sin brought a split in the continuum of the natural and transnatural spheres. Evil caused a rip, a "great gulf" between the material and spiritual dimensions. Rather than consciously moving from one "room" to another, death becomes the means of passage. The time is coming, however, when the physical universe will be restored to its original condition. There will be no break between Heaven and earth, and death will be eliminated.

The example of Paul

As with many older people, Paul had a sense of his approaching death. He wrote to his young protégé, Timothy, these words:

> For I am already being poured out as a drink offering, and the time of my departure has come. I have fought the good fight, I have finished the course, I have kept the faith; in the future there is laid up for me the crown of righteousness, which the Lord, the righteous Judge, will award to me on that day; and not only to me, but also to all who have loved His appearing. (2 Timothy 4:6-8 NASU)

The person in covenant with God, and yielded to the lordship of Jesus Christ, experiences a sense of completion as he or she approaches and enters the death passage.

Paul is conscious of three things as he is nears the death passage. First, he has fought the good fight. Some people experience a sweeping review of their life as they near death. The memories of failures are there, but the focus is drawn to the sweet reflections on battles over temptation and compromise won. The "good fight" is waged on both the personal and corporate levels.

The person cut off from God may feel guilt over personal sins and the way he or she has abused or failed others. But for the individual whose sins have been removed by the blood of Christ, there is no memory of sin, because it's all been wiped out. There's only the awareness during that trip through the death channel of the victories won in and through Christ.

Second, as Paul faces his dying process, he joyfully asserts, "I have finished the course." The person in covenant with Christ lives and breathes purpose. At times he or she may not even know the specifics of that purpose, but they are confident God is carrying it out through them.

Down deep in his misery, Job, through the revelation of the Spirit, declares that a person's "days are determined," and that "the number of his months" is with God. (Job 14:5) The Psalmist understands this as well, and writes,

> The LORD knows the days of the blameless,
> And their inheritance will be forever ...

> Your eyes have seen my unformed substance;
> And in Your book were all written
> The days that were ordained for me,
> When as yet there was not one of them.
> (Psalm 37:18; 139:16 NASU)

God's people know that the number of their days is tied directly to the purpose for which they are placed in the world. Thus, when they are moving through the death channel, there is the peace of knowing the days have ended because the mission is complete, and they can now return Home to Heaven.

"The work of dying well is, in largest part, the work of living well," wrote Richard John Neuhaus, before his own journey through the death passage.[4] Living well means holding to one's course, defined by purpose and mission.

"I have kept the faith," Paul says. He is ready to enter the death passage with security and confidence. Satan has tried every way possible to put a wedge between Paul and God—troubles, pain, humiliation, sacrifice, temptations, emotional distress, constant pulls to give up. Paul knows a collision with Nero is soon inevitable. He knows his dying process might be precipitated by torture, or it may be sudden, through the lopping off of his head. But he passes through with assurance, knowing he has not abandoned the truth.

---

[4] "Born Toward Dying," Richard John Neuhaus, *First Things*, January 8, 2009.

The sense of completion, resolution and triumph give joy and peace to God's people as they journey through the death channel.

The surprising example of Jesus

The fourth example of the passage from the natural to the transnatural realm is somber, eerie—and surprising. It is that of Jesus Himself, in His final moments on the cross. What is surprising is that He is the immaculate incarnation of God, and yet, in this moment, Jesus has assumed the role of history's greatest sinner—becoming "sin for us" (2 Corinthians 5:21). His passage includes a poignant moment that reveals what it's like for someone who is *separated* from God to go through the dying process.

Though Jesus will rise in three earth-days in great victory, He must first endure an eternity of separation from the Father. At one point in His dying process, Jesus is plunged into terror, and cries, "My God, My God, why have you forsaken Me?" Between that desperate question and His final assertion, "It is finished!" is a brief span of earth-time, but an eternity on the time-scale of the spiritual domain. Because He must bear the full load of our guilt and receive all the consequences of our sin, Jesus must be cut off, separated and removed from the presence of God the Father, Who is absolute in His holiness.

In that death channel, Jesus, the atoning Savior, shows the horror of death for the person not in covenant with God.

Thomas Paine, among the American revolutionaries, was a non-believer in Christ and His salvation. He had debunked faith in some of his writings. As he lay dying, Paine reportedly became aware of his separation from God, and would cry out, in what one observer described as "paroxysms of distress," these words, "O Lord, help me! God help me! Jesus Christ help me!" At one point Paine cried that he would "give worlds if I had them" that certain of his books and writings questioning God hadn't been published.

A woman who attended the death of David Hume, the atheist philosopher, said she hoped never to go through anything like that again. At one point, as he neared the death passage, Hume said he had sought for light all his life, and that now he was sinking into the deepest darkness of all.

Beautiful Passage

John Payson's passage through death, gives a glimpse, however, into what we experience as we die safe in Christ. As he died, Payson said,

> "Christ died for me. I am mounting up to the throne of God!" Then breaking forth in rapturous strains of praise, he said: "I know I am dying, but my death-bed is a bed of roses; I have no thorns planted on my dying pillow. Heaven already is begun. I die a safe, easy, happy death. Thou, my God, art present, I

> know, I feel Thou art. Precious Jesus! Glory to God!"

Like my friend, "Brother Bo," the death-bed of this godly man became a pulpit, and his passage through the death-channel a wonderful example of what it's like when people redeemed by Jesus Christ make that journey.

Chapter 2

BEING IS BETTER THAN EXISTENCE

There was only the sense of being wafted high above the earth by a whispering wind. Irene and I felt wonder at the sublime world we had entered.

On a bone-numbing non-stop flight from San Francisco to Hong Kong, my wife and I had been invited to come up to the cockpit of the Boeing-747 jumbo jet that sped us across the Pacific. I had expected a jumble of dials, buttons, levers, read-outs, along with the tense feel of urgency and the searing noise of powerful jet engines. Instead, there was only the sigh of the wind, like that pleasant exhalation we experience when we are at rest. In fact, I was amazed at how relaxed the pilot and co-pilot seemed to be. They sat in big, comfortable chairs surrounded by a surprisingly minimal set of avionics. Coming into the cockpit, Irene and I had passed a door behind which backup crew slept.

Dawn was just awakening across the Pacific Ocean. Its gray demeanor was different only in tone from the water 33,000 or so feet below us. Hong Kong was still two hours ahead—which was a good thing, since the airport didn't open until 6 a.m.

The only thing that rippled my serenity was the awareness that somewhere back there in the night, we had crossed the point of no return. There was an invisible boundary down there on the mountain-waved Pacific that signaled we had completed an important stage of our passage, and that it was impossible to turn back.

This is also the nature of death and dying. When death occurs, we have crossed the point of no return. Dying is the approach to that critical juncture. While we are in the dying process there is the possibility of physical resuscitation and spiritual regeneration.

Beyond the point of no return there is only the fixed movement toward the destination we have chosen—Heaven or Hell.

Being and existence

For the person alive in Christ, dying is the passage into the highest level of being, which God intended for His whole creation.

"Being" and "existence" are separate conditions. Our being is eternal, but existence is as brief as a breath. Being is continuation of the person in the transnatural realm, but existence is living in the natural, finite dimension.

"Existence" is animated by *bios,* the whirring and cranking of the biochemical machines God wired into our bodies. The "inner life" of existence is *psuche,* a Greek word translated "soul," from which we get "psyche" and its word-family. Thinking, feeling and choosing are all functions of the soul.

"Being" is energized by *Zoe*, life as God has and gives. Jesus says, "I am the life (*Zoe*)." (John 14:6) This is because, "as the Father has life (*Zoe*) in Himself, even so He gave to the Son also to have life (*Zoe*) in Himself…" John 5:26)

Therefore, Jesus says He came so that we could "have life, and have it abundantly." (John 10:10) We have His life the moment we receive it into ourselves by receiving Christ.

This is why Paul writes

> And you were dead in your trespasses and sins, in which you formerly walked according to the course of this world, according to the prince of the power of the air, of the spirit that is now working in the sons of disobedience. Among them we too all formerly lived in the lusts of our flesh, indulging the desires of the flesh and of the mind, and were by nature children of wrath, even as the rest. But God, being rich in mercy, because of His great love with which He loved us, even when we were dead in our transgressions, *made us alive together with Christ* (by grace you have been saved), and raised us up with Him, and seated us with Him in the heavenly places in Christ Jesus…" (Ephesians 2:1-6, emphasis added)[5]

---

[5] "Alive," in the Greek original, is *suzoopoieo*, which is based on *zoe*.

This was part of the profound insight God gave my friend Bo Adkison that day at the staff retreat. Bo's shout was over the discovery of his ministry focus for the last phase of his earthly work, but also he caught a glimpse of what dying really is. I was greatly encouraged as I watched Bo enter the passage himself. The same vivid vision of the glory of that crossing with which Bo had comforted so many others brought peace and hope to him on his deathbed.

Other saints of God have seen the same thing.

- In July, 1719, Joseph Addison called for his stepson as he lay dying. "I have sent for you that you may see how a Christian can die," he told the young man.
- John Newton, the converted slave trader who wrote "Amazing Grace" approached the end of his life in 1807, and said, "I am still in the land of the dying; I shall be in the land of the living soon."
- A Chinese Communist executioner was so struck by the valor and peace of the followers of Christ he killed, he tried to find an explanation. "I've seen many of you die," he said to a pastor. "The Christians die differently. What is their secret?"[6]

Defining Death

Birth and death actually have similar characteristics. Birth is an event that is the culmination of a nine-month

---

[6] Retrieved from http://users.belgacom.net/gc674645/grave/lastword.htm

process called gestation. Death is also an event at the end of a process—dying.

Medical science gives us a definition of death centered on the physical. Interestingly, dying words reveal whether a person is existence or being-focused. Humphrey Bogart, for example, said, reportedly, as he was dying, "I should never have switched from Scotch to Martinis."

The Bible gives us the true definition of death. "For then the dust will return to the earth, and the spirit will return to God who gave it." (Ecclesiastes 12:7) The passage notes both the end of existence and the continuation of being. James 2:26 provides the same truth in defining death: "For just as the body without the spirit is dead, so faith without works is also dead." Both passages show that, according to the Bible, our source for understanding the transnatural (as well as the natural) dimension, death occurs in the human being when the person's spirit leaves his or her body.

Thus, the process of dying is the passage of the human spirit from one "place" to another. Further, it's also possible the Bible is showing that biological function doesn't cease until the spirit is gone, and the moment it leaves, biological function stops.[7]

---

[7] Some medical procedures can maintain mechanical function even after the spirit has left the body. Grieving families sometimes prolong that function even after the spirit has departed. "Pulling the plug" is a hard decision, but sometimes when it is clear the person is gone and function is sustained artificially, it is the appropriate decision. What the Bible forbids is *active* measures to bring about death, like abortion and euthanasia. Withdrawing life

Again, the Bible provides important insight through its identification of the body as God's "temple."[8] God created the physical structure of the human body as the dwelling place of His Spirit within the created domain, just as He inspired the construction of the Jerusalem Temple in the Old Covenant era as the "home" of the Ark of Covenant. The manifest presence of the omnipresent God burned with glorious splendor above the gold-sheathed box built by Moses. But when the Ark was no longer in the Holy of Holies the Temple lost its function, and "died." Modern Judaism is no longer focused on the Temple, though some Jews as well as Christians anticipate its restoration.

By reflecting on the nature of the human being prior to the plunge into evil, we can gain valuable insight into the process of dying.

For the person in Christ, the passage from the natural to the transnatural dimension is a restoration to the original, "mint" condition of the human being. Prior to the fall, Adam and Eve had a rich exterior life, but it was controlled completely by an interior life in unbroken communion with God, through His indwelling Holy Spirit.

The inner experience of these pre-fall humans had these functions:

- Continual communion with God

---

support is not an active measure in this sense, unless there is the possibility the person may have chances of recovery.

[8] 1 Corinthians 6:19.

- Conscience that knew instinctively God's Kingdom order
- Intuition based entirely on the Holy Spirit
- Thought informed totally by the Mind of the Logos — the Christ
- Emotions aligned completely with the Holy Spirit of God
- A will set resolutely on the will of the Father

All these functions hummed with perfection, just as they were designed by the Creator. There was no break between the human spirit and the Holy Spirit, and the energy flowing from that uninterrupted linkage fueled the dynamics of thought, feeling, volition and behavior.

In their pre-fall condition, Adam and Eve had perfectly integrated personalities.

Fragmentation and re-integration

Sin fragments the human being.

When Adam and Eve sinned the human spirit died immediately to God and His Kingdom. Because the spirit, which was the core of the unfallen soul, was designed to bring the whole person into linkage and interaction with God in the spiritual dimension, after the entry of evil it was alive only to the kingdom of darkness and the kingdom of self — the world, the flesh and the devil.

The soul gradually was infiltrated with the darkness of the spirit dead to God. The mind began to fall into delusion and wrong thinking. Negative passions seeped, then surged into the emotions. The soul began to assert its own independence and its will was set on its own interests, not the interests of God.

Years ago an ice storm snapped the electric lines connecting our home to the power plant that transmitted electrical energy to us. Thankfully, a neighbor across the street had a large generator, and he ran a line from that temporary power source to our home. But we discovered that the alternate source was no substitute for the power plant. We could operate only a few circuits, and my friend had to keep pouring gasoline into the generator to keep it whirring. Further, the power it sent us was limited.

When the human spirit dies to God, the soul (psyche) becomes the dominant force of the person's inner life. Like the generator, it is an inadequate power source for human living.

As the great quest of physiological science is the cure for cancer, so the highest aim of psychology is the integration of human personality. Strictly "natural" psychology will never achieve this goal because it ignores the rending reality of sin. Psychologists whose view of the human is based on the Bible understand this.

Paul Tournier was an acclaimed Swiss psychotherapist who was also a committed Christian. "Man is not just a body and a mind," he wrote, but "a spiritual being. It is impossible to know him if one disregards his deepest reality." Tournier understood well the fragmentation of human personality, and wrote

> "It is an unscientific assumption of materialist philosophy which supposes that material facts (anatomical and physiological) are the cause, and that moral (psychological and spiritual) facts are the consequences, and not the other way about."[9]

Dr. Karl Menninger's insight about the linkage of evil and fragmentation was so great he wrote a book whose title revealed his concern, *Whatever Became of Sin?* Sin, he said, had been externalized into a social or cultural problem rather than a person's violation of God's absolute standard of rightness. The externalization of sin led to blame, not responsibility. Further, if sin does not exist, neither does guilt. There can never be true resolution in the inner person for, according to contemporary culture there is nothing "wrong" and nothing to "confess."

Yet fragmentation is a reality experienced by every human being. Spirit, soul and body are at war with one another, with each seeking the dominant role. Even an atheist like Freud realized this. The higher self—the *super-ego*—was embattled by the forces of the *ego* and the lowest facet of personality, the *id*. The *id*, Freud taught, operates by the "pleasure principle," and is a chaotic force seeking one

---

[9] Retrieved from http://www.absoluteastronomy.com/topics/Paul_Tournier.

thing—instant gratification. The "reality principle" guides the *ego* to find realistic ways to satisfy the demands of the *id*, in line with the moral force of the *super-ego*.

Fragmentation is an event that occurs in the fall, but an ongoing process in every person that can culminate in insanity. Fragmentation is the opposite of sanctification. In fragmentation, the spirit dies to God and the darkened soul becomes the predominate expression of the inner life of the individual without God. The spiritual death of the human spirit spreads into the soul, and ultimately into the body

In sanctification, the human spirit, made alive in Christ through justification, and indwelt by the Holy Spirit gradually becomes the predominate expression of the inner life of the person. Spiritual life spreads into the soul, and culminates in the body through dying, which brings the redeemed human being into the new body, with the glory of Christ's resurrection Body

Therefore, justification is an *event* that happens at the level of the human spirit, sanctification is a *process* that occurs in the soul, and glorification is an *event* that happens in the body.

Dying is the re-integration of the personality of the redeemed human being. The veil between soul and spirit is torn down just as the curtain of the Temple separating the Holy of Holies from the rest was rent from top to bottom at Jesus' death on the cross.

There is a twofold meaning in this business about the Temple veil. First, it symbolizes that the way to God is opened to sinful human beings through Christ's atonement.

The tearing of the veil also symbolizes that the fragmentation of human personality is healed through the salvation in Jesus Christ, the Lord. The functions of the soul (a process begun in the soul at conversion and regeneration) are now joined perfectly to the spirit, which is indwelt by the Holy Spirit, and the fragmentation is ended.

In fact, one of the meanings of the Greek word for "salvation"—*soteria*—is inner well-being, health and preservation. This is why Paul writes, in 1 Thessalonians 5:23,

> "… may the God of peace Himself sanctify you entirely; and may your spirit and soul and body be *preserved complete*, without blame at the coming of our Lord Jesus Christ." (Emphasis added)

Thus the person dying in Christ experiences nothing but the pure thoughts of God—the "knowing fully" Paul refers to in 1 Corinthians 13:12—along with the undiluted peace and joy of the Holy Spirit.

Foundational authority

The Biblical basis for this understanding of the dying process is revealed in a surprising way. Just as the *microcosm*—the individual human being—undergoes a dying process, so the *megacosm*—the created universe—will undergo a dying process; therefore, to understand the dying process for the microcosm of the individual human being, we study the dying process of the megacosm.

There are important Greek words embedded in the Scripture by the Holy Spirit that inform our understanding of the megacosmic dying process by which we can understand the passage of the individual human being

Paliggenesia

This beautiful word appears in Matthew 19:28, when Jesus speaks of "the regeneration when the Son of Man will sit on His glorious throne." *Paliggenesia* is also the term in Titus 3:5, referring to "the washing of regeneration."

These two uses of the Greek word reveal two levels of application. In Matthew, Jesus is referring to the regeneration of the megacosm—the universe. Titus 3:5 uses the word in relation to the microcosm of the human being. Therefore, *paliggenesia* shows the correlation between the passage of both the *"mega"* and the *"micro"* into a new state of being. The picture and process for the passing of the universe and the individuals within it are the same.

Paliggenesia "is also applied to designate both the great geological changes which the earth has undergone and the transformations in the insect kingdom, such as of caterpillars into butterflies," says a scholarly commentary.[10]

---

[10] McClintock and Strong Encyclopedia, Electronic Database. Copyright © 2000, 2003 by Biblesoft, Inc.

Paliggenesia means "renewal to a higher level of existence," according to the *Theological Dictionary of the New Testament*.[11] This is not reincarnation, or merely a return to the "same old-same old" existence prior to the passage into a new quality of being. Rather, *paliggenesia* is a crossing over into "new heavens and a new earth, in which righteousness dwells." (2 Peter 3:13)

Thayer's Greek Lexicon focuses on *paliggenesia* as referring to a restoration to an original condition.[12] With respect to a redeemed human being, *paliggenesia* is the return of the "primal and perfect" state that existed before Adam and Eve opened human nature to sin. The dying process is a metamorphosis (Greek for "change of form") in which a human being existing in the natural dimension is transformed into a being living eternally in the transnatural domain.

Apokatastasis

Not long after the Holy Spirit's energizing of Jesus' disciples on the Day of Pentecost, Peter and John go the Temple for Sabbath prayer. They encounter a crippled man, and God heals him through them.

The man's exuberant response draws a crowd. The people are goggle-eyed in amazement. Peter's confidence and passion for the Gospel have been ignited in the events of

---

[11] Kittel and Bromiley, *Theological Dictionary of the New Testament,* Grand Rapids: Wm. B. Eerdmans Publishing Company, Volume I, page 686.
[12] Thayer's Greek Lexicon, Electronic Database. Copyright (c) 2000 by Biblesoft

Christ's resurrection and Pentecost, and, with boldness, he speaks to the mass:

> "... repent and return, so that your sins may be wiped away, in order that times of refreshing may come from the presence of the Lord; and that He may send Jesus, the Christ appointed for you, whom heaven must receive until the period of *restoration of all things* about which God spoke by the mouth of His holy prophets from ancient time." (Acts 3:19-21, emphasis added)

"Restoration" is the translation of the Greek, *apokatastasis*, a second word that gives a biblical foundation for understanding the human dying process. The term as used in the Bible signifies the restoration of the whole cosmos to its pre-fall state.[13] The dying process is therefore a passage into the cosmos as it was prior to the entry of evil (which is the way the world will be forever).

This fallen age is but a moment in the history of the cosmos, and so is our life in it. God's cosmic plan is to bring everything back to its original state of perfection and glory—including us as human beings, and dying for the redeemed person is part of it.

Dying, for the person in Christ, is the passage into that new quality of life! This is Paul's point when he writes, in Romans 6:5, "if we have become united with Him in the

---

[13] Thayer's Greek Lexicon, Electronic Database. Copyright (c) 2000 by Biblesoft

likeness of His death, certainly we shall also be in the likeness of His resurrection..." The dying process is an acceleration of what starts in a person the moment he or she receives Christ and His unique quality of life. "But we all, with unveiled face," Paul continues, in 2 Corinthians 3:18, "beholding as in a mirror the glory of the Lord, are being transformed into the same image from glory to glory, just as from the Lord, the Spirit."

Further, while we are in the time-space-matter dimension and the body designed to function within it,

> "we groan under the burden and sigh deeply (weighed down, depressed, oppressed) — not that we want to put off the body (the clothing of the spirit), but rather that we would be further clothed, so that what is mortal (our dying body) may be swallowed up by life [after the resurrection]. (2 Corinthians 5:4 AMP)

Therefore, it's only logical that Paul would declare his consuming desire regarding Christ is to

> "know Him and the power of His resurrection and the fellowship of His sufferings, being conformed to His death; in order that I may attain to the resurrection from the dead. (Philippians 3:10-11 NASU)

In this world, sanctification is the means by which the soul begins its journey toward restoration and wholeness. Dying, for the person in Christ, is the means by which the body begins its journey toward restoration and the glory of God through resurrection.

Both processes require dying.

The soul must die to itself so that it might receive Zoe, the true life of God, through His Son, Jesus Christ. The body must die so that the physical being can be clothed with a physical structure fit for the transnatural dimension—the resurrection body.

At justification, which occurs at the moment of salvation, we enter the *fact* of Christ's Resurrection. In glorification, which comes through dying, we enter the *experience* of Christ's Resurrection.

Parerchomai

The third New Testament Greek word that provides rich insight into the dying process is the primary term from which we get some of the most popular colloquialisms for death, "pass," or "pass on."

Peter uses *parerchomai* in 2 Peter 3:10, which says,

> … the day of the Lord will come like a thief, in which the heavens will *pass away* with a roar and the elements will be destroyed with intense heat, and the earth and its works will be burned up. (Emphasis added)

Parerchomai means "to come to be present at a particular place"[14] It carries the idea of leaving one place and arriving at another. The term also signifies approaching a particular location.[15] In the process of dying, then, the individual in Christ is crossing the boundary between two different dimensions of substance and time.

Henry Van Dyke (1852-1933) perhaps captured the meaning of *parerchomai* and the description of the dying process more accurately and beautifully than any modern writer, when he put it like this:

> I am standing upon the seashore. A ship at my side spreads her white sails to the morning breeze and starts for the blue ocean. She is an object of beauty and strength. I stand and watch her until at length she hangs like a speck of white cloud just where the sea and sky come to mingle with each other.
>
> Then someone at my side says: "There, she is gone!"
>
> "Gone where?"
>
> Gone from my sight. That is all. She is just as large in mast and hull and spar as she was when she left my side and she is just as able to

---

[14] Greek-English Lexicon Based on Semantic Domain. Copyright (c) 1988 United Bible Societies, New York.

[15] Biblesoft's New Exhaustive Strong's Numbers and Concordance with Expanded Greek-Hebrew Dictionary. Copyright © 1994, 2003 Biblesoft, Inc. and International Bible Translators, Inc.)

bear her load of living freight to her destined port.

Her diminished size is in me, not in her. And just at the moment when someone at my side says: "There, she is gone!" there are other eyes watching her coming, and other voices ready to take up the glad shout: 'Here she comes!'"

And that is dying.

PART 2
YOUR PASSAGE

Chapter 3

WHERE IS HEAVEN?

When you take your first step in Heaven, where do you go? Is it far away or near? If it is close by does that explain the alleged appearances of deceased loved ones?

On what Winston Churchill called a certain "foggy afternoon" in November, 1947, he was attempting to copy a damaged portrait of his long-dead father. Churchill was in his art studio at Chartwell, his home.

I have stood in that studio, and felt the atmosphere soaked still in the memory of Churchill. I have tried to feel what Churchill must have felt, and understand how comforting this retreat in a little building several hundred yards from the main house must have been for Sir Winston. But there was one experience Churchill had there that I could neither desire nor expect to enter into.

"I was just trying to give the twirl to his moustache when I suddenly felt an odd sensation," wrote Churchill later. He spun around and saw his father, Randolph, who had died 50 years earlier. "He was so exactly like my memories of him in his most charming moods that I could hardly believe my eyes," Sir Winston recalled. Though he wasn't afraid, Churchill said he decided to "stand where I was and go no further."

Was Churchill's vision of his father the hallucination of an aged mind, weary from the stresses of almost superhuman challenges? Was it the dream manufactured in the slumber of a gray day? Was it possible it was even a demonic delusion? Was it reality? Where was Randolph Churchill? Where did he come from?

While it would be easy to conclude that this was merely the dream aroused from the subconscious of an old man in drifting sleep on a gray and chilly afternoon, there is no doubt that many people have felt the presence of loved ones after death. C.S. Lewis reported experiencing the company of his recently deceased wife, Joy, and J.B. Phillips, the great Bible translator said C.S. Lewis came to him after Lewis' death. General George Patton, pinned down by enemy fire at Argonne in World War I, said he saw his deceased grandfather and great-uncles looking at him from the sky, a vision that inspired Patton to rally an infantry and tank assault on the adversaries. In World War II Patton said his father, who had died in 1927, visited him in his tent, and encouraged him for the coming battles.

Some people see the Bible as aiding and abetting what the materialists would call sheer fantasy. They argue that this confirms that the Bible is itself a collection of wild imaginings. Actually, it is all those worldviews that deny evil, the sinful nature of the human being, and the outcomes of falling short of God's glory that thrive on delusion and fantasy.

Fantasy concocts all the imaginations about Heaven that reject the Bible's revelation of it—especially those wild concepts about where Heaven is.

One of the patriarchs of atheology—the theology of atheism—is Friedrich Nietzsche, the 19th century German philosopher who gave us "god-is-dead" theory as well as the concept of "superman" and the will to power as the driving force of human dynamics. Nietzsche, drunk with hubris, also felt he knew where Heaven is: "The 'kingdom of Heaven' is a condition of the heart, not something that comes 'upon the earth' or 'after death,'" he pronounced.

Omar Khayyam the mystic was on the opposite end of the metaphysical spectrum from Friedrich Nietzsche the atheistic existentialist. But, like the non-believer the mystic felt he knew where Heaven is also:

> "I sent my Soul through the Invisible,
> Some letter of that After life to spell:
> And by and by my Soul return'd to me,
> And answer'd: 'I Myself am Heav'n and Hell"

That is truly grim news!

Henry David Thoreau got it a little better when he said "Heaven is under our feet as well as over our heads."

But the question I pose for all who would reject biblical belief is this: *Why would I put the hope and trust for my eternal destiny and that of my loved ones upon the authority of these finite, immanent sources... even the best of them?*

The Bible is hard reality because it is honest enough to include Thomas and his choleric questioning. Jesus tells His disciples in John 14 that He is going away and preparing a place for them and will come back and get them. Further, Jesus tells them that they know the way where He is going. "How can we know the way to be with you when we don't even know where you are going?" queries Thomas.

Analytical Thomas doesn't know the "where" and if he doesn't know that he certainly doesn't know the "way"!

So where is Heaven? Can we really know where it is?

Before we can try to answer, "Where is Heaven?" we must first ask another: "What is a 'where'?" From the perspective of our universe, the "spacetime universe", a "where" is a *place* in space existing in kronos-time. But there is a huge problem here. Astrophysics, carried along by Einstein's theories of Special and General Relativity, show that both time and space and all their properties and laws came into being at the moment of creation.

There was no space before the Big Bang or whatever we call it, and there was no time. Yet if God inhabits eternity, how could there be a "where" and a time for His existence? And if Heaven is infinite, or eternal, where could there be a place and time for it to exist?

Without intending to the physicists themselves are answering the question. The findings lead to the conclusion that, as Dinesh D'Souza puts it, "space, time, and the laws of physics are local to our universe," and that any realms that exist beyond our universe "could operate independently of our conceptions of space and time altogether." That would help explain the appearances of Jesus after His resurrection, when space and time were not obstructions to His movement. "Now suddenly we see the coherence of the Christian concept of eternity, a realm beyond space and time and the known laws of science," writes D'Souza.[16]

Looking for Heaven

When we start looking for Heaven our first inclination is to look up. Therefore the first step we must take in our search for the "where" of Heaven is to come to terms with the spatial terms. Thus it all depends on what "up" is.

Genesis 1:1 tells us that "in the beginning God created the heavens and the earth." In Genesis 1:17 we discover that God put the moon and the stars "in the expanse of the heavens" to give us light. When, in Psalm 8:3, the Psalmist says that when he contemplates God's "heavens, the work of Your fingers, the moon and the stars" the writer is referring to the natural universe, the one we see when we look up physically.

There is therefore a distinction between "the heavens" and Heaven, and therefore a difference in the association of "up" with regard to each. The dissimilarity is in the nuance of distinction between the qualitative and the quantitative.

When I look "up" to "the heavens" I do so with my physical eyes, but when I look "up" to Heaven I do so with

---
[16] Dinesh D'Souza, *Life After Death*, 82.

the eyes of my spirit whose sight is given by the indwelling Holy Spirit. When I do so I look into an entirely different cosmos. Owen Gingerich, an astronomer, says that

> "Christians have long envisioned a world with which they have no physical contact, not the heavens, but Heaven, the empyrean.[17] It is a totally other place, without evil and suffering, and where the inhabitants never grow old. It thus cannot be our present world remodeled, for the remodeling would strike at the very heart of all our physical understanding. To suspend the rules of our cosmos would be tantamount to being in another universe."[18]

This does not mean therefore that Heaven is not tangible. We have already seen that in Heaven there is a new type of body functioning in the context of a new quality of physics. At some point on the kronos-timeline this new physics that is already the reality in the kairos-continuum will overwhelm the old physics of the world we presently inhabit. Gingerich is right: it won't be a "remodeled" world but a completely new world in the original, pre-fall condition of earth and its universe. While we are in this body we see with the eyes of finitude, and therefore cannot see the infinite with that limited seeing.

---

[17] "Empyrean": The highest extent of Heaven; the place of the Throne of God
[18] D'Souza, *op. cit.,* 88.

But we can see Heaven with the eyes of faith, and that produces a hope and lifestyle of the highest quality. Several Scriptures remind us of this:

- 1 Corinthians 15:19   *If we have hoped in Christ in this life only, we are of all men most to be pitied.*
- Titus 2:11-13   *For the grace of God has appeared, bringing salvation to all men, instructing us to deny ungodliness and worldly desires and to live sensibly, righteously and godly in the present age, looking for the blessed hope and the appearing of the glory of our great God and Savior, Christ Jesus...*
- 1 Peter 1:3   *Blessed be the God and Father of our Lord Jesus Christ, who according to His great mercy has caused us to be born again to a living hope through the resurrection of Jesus Christ from the dead...*

The qualitative lift of the reality of Heaven has been noted by those who across history have looked for the "where" through the eyes of the Spirit. Ignatius of Antioch as he was being martyred said, "It is better for me to die in behalf of Jesus Christ than to reign over all the ends of the earth." Matthew Henry wrote that "(h)e whose head is in heaven need not fear to put his feet into the grave."

Steve Jobs, the sire and master of Apple Computers, the progenitor of the I-Phone, the I-Pad, and all things "I" embraced a California-postmodern form of Buddhism. But even he could see whatever is beyond the grave as a kind of "upgrade" as computer-speak might describe it. Cancer was advancing in his body and death was closing in when he spoke these words:

> No one wants to die. Even people who want to go to heaven don't want to die to get there. And yet death is the destination we all share. No one has ever escaped it. And that is as it should be, because Death is very likely the single best invention of Life. It is Life's change agent. It clears out the old to make way for the new.

As a quasi-Buddhist Jobs had no hope of Heaven, just the hope of getting out of the way to give room for the "new".

But perhaps my favorite quote about the qualitative lift of Heaven is from C.S. Lewis: "Aim at heaven and you will get earth thrown in. Aim at earth and you get neither."

Yet Thomas' question still lingers, and even becomes desperate when we lose a cherished person: Where are You going? Where is the "place" You are preparing for us? How far "beyond" is the "great Beyond"?

Please tell us where Heaven is in terms we can understand on this finite scale!

Expanding the search-area

To search for the "where" on the quantitative-immanent scale of finite space and kronos-time we have to broaden our range of search. Flesh and blood can neither truly understand it nor even know how to look. But God is love and love wants to communicate, so God gives us tantalizing evidences across Scripture that provide limited (the limitations are on our part, not God's) glimpses of where Heaven might be. By the way, this is why we are not using Near Death Experiences (NDEs) as primary sources in this study—they give us only the limited human view.

Therefore, in our quest for the "where" of Heaven, let's expand the search zone. There are so many examples in the Bible of people on earth interacting with heavenly phenomena that we can't list them all. But let's look just at those interactions that were not based on visions or dreams (like "Jacob's Ladder") but on interactions on the level of the immanent and physical.

Theophanies and Christophanies in general

Phaneroo in the Greek New Testament means to make that which is invisible and hidden visible to human eyes. This is a visible, physical manifestation, and is therefore not a vision or dream. *Theos* means "God" and *Christos* is "Christ". Therefore a *Theophany* is an appearance of the totality of the Godhead to human eyes and a *Christophany* is a manifestation of Christ primarily before His Incarnation in Jesus of Nazareth.

Hagar, Sarah's banished servant, experienced a Theophany, as well as Abraham, Moses, Jacob, and other Old Testament people. That "Fourth Man" in the fiery furnace with Daniel's three friends could be categorized as a

Christophany since He came to rescue or be "savior" to them in the midst of the flames.

Because God dwells in the "highest heaven" and because Christ is the Second Person of the Heaven-enthroned Trinity, any Theophany or Christophany is a break-through of Heaven into the finite world.

Moses on Sinai

The destiny-setting appearance of God to Moses in the Burning Bush was a Theophany, but something that went beyond it happened when Moses received the Law on Sinai. The fact this was an experience on the physical, tangible level (as was the Burning Bush on a more limited scale) is evidenced in what happened when he came down. Exodus 34:29-35 reports that Moss' face shown so brightly—though he was not aware—that the people were afraid to approach him.

When Ezekiel sees a vision of God enthroned in Heaven the whole atmosphere, including God Himself, appeared to Ezekiel's comprehension as "glowing metal." (Ezekiel 1:27) Centuries later, in the Revelation visions, John sees Christ as having eyes like "a flame of fire" and feet appearing as bronze still glowing from the burnishing fires. (Revelation 1:12-16)

Since Moses' physical face is glowing, and is discernible by human eyes to the point he has to veil his countenance, it is clear that up on Sinai, kronos (earth/natural-time) and kairos (Heaven/eternal-time) have converged, meaning the Infinity of Heaven has broken through into the finitude of the natural physical world.

The Mount of Transfiguration

There is a similar experience to that of Moses on Sinai when Jesus takes Peter, James, and John to the top of Mount Tabor—except on an even grander scale. Matthew 17:2 reports that Jesus was "transfigured" before them.

"Transfigured" is, in Greek, *metamorphoo*, from *meta* ("change") and *morphos* ("form"). Jesus appears to Peter, James, and John, in His essence, pure *Zoe*, which is His true and heavenly Form stripped of its *bios* shell.

Further, Matthew 17:2 gives us another familiar clue that in the Transfiguration experience Heaven has broken into space and kronos-time: Jesus' face shone like the sun, and His garments became as white as light." But there's even more: Peter, James, and John see Moses and Elijah with Jesus. Somehow these figures from past history have been allowed to bridge the gap between kronos and kairos, and appear in kronos-observable form.

Peter's reaction tells us everything: He has actually seen something so spectacular and unique that he doesn't want to leave but stay and build grand monuments that would mark the spot in space where kronos-time seemed to be overcome and beings from the past actually were present in the existential moment.

Christ's post-resurrection appearances

It's clear as we examine Christ's post-resurrection appearances that we are seeing a Person from a realm where the properties and laws of our universe are of no effect. As we look closely at just three of appearances we get hints about "where" Heaven is by a reverse methodology of observing where it is *not* bound by earthly restrictions.

John 20:19 shows us that "where" Heaven is there are no spatial boundaries as we experience them in earth. On the evening of Resurrection Day, the disciples had holed up behind tightly locked doors for fear of the people who had crucified Jesus. Yet suddenly Jesus "came and stood in their midst." Bolted doors and walls were no problem for the dimension in which Jesus' heavenly body functioned.

John 21 shows that Jesus' new form transcended time as well as space. The disciples had returned to Galilee and their fishing nets. It would have taken Jesus' followers many days to trek the more than 70 miles, but Jesus was already there.

The post-resurrection experiences demonstrate that "where" Heaven is there is a new form of "biology". Though Jesus' new body was unhampered by time and space, it could still function in those dimensions, but obviously at a higher level. He caught fish, and ate with His men from Galilee, and also sat for supper with followers from Emmaus. While Jesus would not permit Mary and others to touch Him in the sense of clinging to Him and trying to hold Him back, He did allow them to touch His wounds.

Therefore based on the resurrection appearances of Jesus we would conclude that "where" Heaven is is outside the spatial-temporal-material boundaries of our universe. He transcended the physical properties of the spacetime universe, and the laws of natural physics. Wherever Heaven "is" it is not within the universe we inhabit, yet "near" enough for there to be inter-dimensional interaction.

And wherever Heaven is, Jesus' intention is that all people who identify with Him as His followers live there with Him, as He tells His friends while preparing them for His departure from earth.

A closer look at John 14:1-6

"Do not let your heart be troubled; believe in God, believe also in Me. In My Father's house are many dwelling places; if it were not so, I would have told you; for I go to prepare a place for you. If I go and prepare a place for you, I will come again and receive you to Myself, that where I am, *there* you may be also. And you know the way where I am going." Thomas said to Him, 'Lord, we do not know where You are going, how do we know the way?' Jesus said to him, "I am the way, and the truth, and the life; no one comes to the Father but through Me."

First, note Jesus' words, "My Father's house." The Greek term for "house" is *oikia,* referring not only to a person's residence, but also that of his or her whole family. The related word, *oikos,* also encompassed a person's possessions. Jesus is therefore describing Heaven, the dwelling of God as a "family compound" where all His offspring live and share the Father's possessions.

I realize that using "compound" might infer a place with boundaries. The idea is appropriate because there is an "outside" with respect to Heaven as Revelation 22:15 makes clear when it says, "Outside are the dogs and the sorcerers and the immoral persons and the murderers and the idolaters, and everyone who loves and practices lying." Those in Christ, however, live in Heaven in and with Jesus Christ, the *only begotten* of the Father, and are His "co-heirs". (Romans 8:17, *et al.*)

Second, Jesus says there are many dwelling places in this vast family compound. The King James translation says "mansions," but "dwelling places" is more accurate. The Greek, *monay* (phonetic spelling) is from *meno,* "to dwell". The term also relates to *monos,* meaning "one" or "single." Jesus is emphasizing that Heaven is not a dormitory where we live with strangers, but is personal as well as relational. This means we retain our uniqueness and individuality in Heaven.

Let's pull together all the clues we have seen in this brief survey and see what they tell us about *where* Heaven is.

Conclusions about the 'where' of Heaven
1. Heaven is beyond us dimensionally but near us spatially.

Movie-makers today relish the wonderful technology called CGI (computer-generated imagery). The skilled technicians can create landscapes, cities, animals, people, and entire worlds. After fashioning CGI "humans" the cyber-wizards can animate them, giving them the appearance of life and action.

The little people, however, are two-dimensional, and this helps us understand what we mean by Heaven being beyond us dimensionally bur near us spatially. The CGI "creator" is in a dimension of greater "weight" than that of the CGI-creature. For one thing, the technician fashioning the image out of electronic impulses lives in the dimension of depth or thickness as well as length and width. But the computer technician is as near the CGI-creature as I am to the computer on which I write these words.

So, as Jesus' appearances show us, though Heaven is an entirely different realm, operating with completely different dimensionality, it is close to us. Jesus makes the point in John 14 when He describes the infrastructure of His Father's House as "dwelling places." Death for the person in Christ is not being projected out to the remote edge of the universe, but is more like moving from the kitchen to the den, or parlor to bedroom.

No wonder we sometimes experience the nearness of our loved ones!

2. The Transcendent Heaven will occasionally break in on the immanent plane.

There is something far more wonderful, even, than post-death encounters with deceased family and friends, and that is *the Incarnation of the Christ in Jesus of Nazareth*. This is the most stunning event in the history of the universe, the ultimate breakthrough of Heaven into the spacetime universe.

Paul tells us in Philippians 2 that to carry out His earthly mission, Jesus laid aside important properties of His Heavenly Being. He became capable of weariness, and, ultimately, death. Yet He could still reach into the dimension of Heaven and nullify the physical properties and laws of our universe, producing what we call "miracles." Jesus could heal lepers, open blind eyes, make paralyzed people walk, and even raise the dead. Every healing in the here-and-now is therefore Heaven breaking into our world. That includes those amazing works that come through medicine and physicians, since all truth arises from God, including that of chemistry and medical skills.

Angelic visitations are breakthroughs of the Heavenly dimension into earth space and time. Angels are "all ministering spirits, sent out to render service for the sake of those who will inherit salvation," says Hebrews 1:14. Most of these angelic interventions are unseen, but on rare occasions they break into our experience. The reason the angels help us but usually stay hidden is that if we saw them we would worship them!

Sometimes God will give us an awareness of a deceased loved one. Any appearance to our mental, emotional, or even physical senses of a friend or family member who has crossed to Heaven can be viewed as authentic when God is the focus of the experience.

3. These breakthroughs are brought about by God sovereignly, and are not be conjured by humans.

King Saul's greatest mistake was when he asked the witch of Endor to "bring up" the prophet Samuel, who was dead. In fact, the decision cost Saul his kingdom. Saul's earlier arrogance and disobedience had quenched the Holy Spirit, on Whom Saul depended for guidance. When Samuel was alive, that direction often came through him, but Saul was cut off from the Spirit because of his sin, and desperately needed direction. So, the witch conducted a séance, and Samuel appeared.

Was this really Samuel? If so, does that mean mediums have the power to summon the dead from the "where" of Heaven? There is nothing in Scripture to indicate it was not Samuel. God apparently permitted this experience to allow Samuel to speak one last time into Saul's life. And what Samuel spoke was judgment.

This was a sovereign act of God, and Scripture strongly forbids humans to take the initiative in seeking communion with those who've gone on into eternity. Moses had long ago given God's command on this subject:

> … "do not let your people practice fortune-telling or sorcery, or allow them to interpret omens, or engage in witchcraft, or cast spells, or function as mediums or psychics, or call forth the spirits of the dead. Anyone who does these things is an object of horror and disgust to the LORD." (Deuteronomy 18:10-12 NLT)

Peter Kreeft writes that

> The reason for the stricture is probably protection against the danger of deception by evil spirits. We are out of our depth, our knowledge, our control once we open the doors to the supernatural. The only openings that are safe for us are the ones God has approved: revelation, prayer, His own miracles (Catholics would also believe the Sacraments) ... and primarily Christ Himself... The danger is not physical but spiritual, and spiritual danger always centers on deception. The Devil is "a liar and the father of lies." (John 8:44) He disguises himself "as an angel of light." (2 Corinthians 11:14)

This is also why I am cautious about an overuse of NDEs—"near-death experiences"—in teaching and counseling.

4. There is an experiential impact on humans existing in the immanent kronos universe who encounter beings inhabiting the transcendent kairos Realm.

My mother and father married in 1935. By the time I came along in 1941 turbulence had already entered their relationship. They divorced in 1951. But later in life, long after my father had died and mother was in early stages of what would become severe dementia, it became evident how deep their love was. She would hear his name, and say, "I loved him so much..."

One afternoon many years ago I was grilling hamburgers behind the garage. Two empty yard chairs sat over by the fence. Suddenly I had the awareness of my mother and father sitting there, holding hands, watching me cook, enjoying the moment with me. I had not been thinking about them, but was focused on getting the burgers done. The awareness came "out of the blue". I did not see them, but just had a spontaneous, unexpected delightful, comforting sense of their presence.

More than a decade later I feel the peace and joy of that moment, and the certainty that my mother and father are in Heaven, together. I realize the moment could have been created in and through my subconscious longing. But that does not explain the transcendent peace and assurance of their wellbeing I feel even as I write these words.

5. Humans are not to replace intimacy, worship, and interaction with God with intimacy, worship, and interaction with beings who may be manifest in a convergence of Heaven and earth brought about by God.

Consider, for example, the "Queen of Heaven" apparitions that seem to break into our dimension at certain places and times. These appearances intrigue and even seem to inspire some Catholics and non-Catholics alike. Our Lady of Fatima, the Virgin of Guadalupe, and other apparitions thought to be manifestations of Mary, the mother of Jesus, are important elements in the folklore of non-biblical spirituality.

The "Queen of Heaven" concept has been around a long time. The ancient Babylonians venerated Ishtar, who would be known in later periods as Venus. Semitic people in antiquity worshipped Ishtar as Astarte. Every historic period seems to have had a "mother goddess" concept. They are all part of a broader idea that those who live in the "where" of Heaven can represent us before the God of Heaven. So, in Catholicism, Mary is a *mediatrix*. Jesus wins our salvation, but Mary intercedes for us, according to the doctrine.

Many therefore conclude that they can look to deceased loved ones to represent them before the Throne of Heaven. Ancestor worship, séances, New Age practices, and other phenomena arise from this belief. But they all fall under the bans of Deuteronomy 18 because they lead many into communion with demons.

Necromancy, or communicating with the dead is strongly warned against in Scripture. Leviticus 19:31 forbids consultations with mediums and necromancers. Deuteronomy 18:9-12 refers to the practice as "abomination." 1 John 4:1 exhorts people to "test every spirit" to make sure they are from God. Revelation 21:8 includes the "sorcerers" among those evil powers cast into the Lake of Fire.

We are not to interact with beings who seem to come to us from the "Great Beyond." It truly is that because it is outside our universe. And yet it is as near to us as my wife is at this moment when I am in my study writing these words and she is in another room of the same house.

Spiritually, the moment we are "born again" in Christ we are born into "citizenship" in Heaven (Philippians 3:20), we are "seated with Christ in heavenly places" (Ephesians 2:6) and are therefore in the same "household" as all the "saints" (Ephesians 2:19), including our deceased loved ones who trusted Christ for their eternal salvation.

Therefore, to open ourselves to anything less than the Transcendent, Singular, absolutely holy God is to commune with the powers of the "outside," the abode of those who rejected relationship with the Father, celebrated by the Psalmist in these words from Psalm 8:1 (emphasis added):

O LORD, our Lord,
How majestic is Your name in all the earth,
Who have displayed Your splendor *above the heavens*!

Chapter 4

STEPPING OUT, STEPPING IN THE NEW BODY

When you die you step out of your old body and step into your new heavenly body. Dying for the person in Christ is like dropping old clothing to the floor and pulling on brand new garments over your head, simultaneously!

But wait: Doesn't the Bible speak of a sequence of putting on the resurrection body? What does it mean that the dead are "asleep" until the coming again of Christ when they are "caught up... to meet the Lord in the air?" (1 Thessalonians 4:17) Wouldn't that infer we are in some sort of suspended state until Christ returns to the earth? Purgatory, maybe?

We'll come to those questions about the "present-future" sequence in a moment. First, let's look at the important revelation the Holy Spirit gives the Apostle Paul about how all this happens:

> "For indeed while we are in this tent, we groan, being burdened, because we do not want to be unclothed but to be clothed, so that what is mortal will be swallowed up by life...this perishable must put on the imperishable, and this mortal must put on

immortality." (2 Corinthians 5:4; NASU; 1 Corinthians 15:53 NKJV)

Peter Kreeft notes that there are at least five ways humanity has tried to understand what we will be after death:[19]

1. Materialism says we are annihilated. There is nothing for us after death. We are extinct.
2. Myth says we survive death as ghosts, mere shadows of what we were.
3. Reincarnation thinks we come back to earth in some other category of mortal body—another person, or perhaps an animal.
4. Platonism teaches the natural immortality of the soul. Death liberates the pure spirit from the body, and we exist in an angelic form.
5. Hinduism and Buddhism believe that only our consciousness survives after death, but it is "cosmic consciousness," not our individual awareness.

"Only in Christianity do we become more than we were before death," says Kreeft. "It is the startling, surprising idea of a new, greater resurrected body." We know this because, as C.S. Lewis wrote, the Bible shows "Christ as passing after death (as no one had passed before) neither into a purely 'spiritual' mode of existence nor into a 'natural' life, but into a life which has its own, new Nature…"[20]

---

[19] Peter Kreeft, *Everything You Ever Wanted to Know About Heaven,* Ignatius Press.
[20] C.S. Lewis, *Miracles,* cited in Kreeft.

Further, if Christ is the "new Adam" then He has the perfect physicality of the old Adam's pre-sin body. Christ's resurrection body was not a "resuscitated" body like that of Lazarus, but a new kind of body that would be appropriate to the atmosphere and environment of Heaven. If we are in Christ, "we will be like Him," says 1 John 3:2.

Thank God He has our special "clothing" waiting for us to step into because most of us know the dread of arriving in some special place dressed inappropriately!

Ill-attired at the Kennedy Center

When I think of the wrong clothes, wrong place, wrong time, my mind goes back to January 20, 1973.

It is midnight, and Irene and I, attired in formal garb, stroll out of Washington's Kennedy Center to our car for the drive back to our home in the Virginia suburbs. The bitter January cold slaps us as we step outside. The Potomac River just behind us is littered with ice. But our thoughts and emotions are still warm from the event celebrating the inauguration of President Richard Nixon's second term.

We had enjoyed a sumptuous dinner, then entered the Kennedy Center's great concert hall. As a member of Nixon's staff I had been given choice seats down front. Irene and I had sat near Henry Kissinger and other luminaries. We had watched and listened as Van Cliburn played a piano concerto, Charlton Heston read a dramatic piece, and Broadway star Pearl Bailey filled the room with her amazing voice.

Up there behind us in his special box, the President, his wife, members of his family and other celebrities took in the scene as we in the audience stole glances of them.

Not even the Washington winter can freeze our delight over the evening as we walk out of the Kennedy Center happily threading our way through the line-up of black limousines. We must hurry home, grab a few hours' sleep, then head back to the heart of the capital for the inaugural parade, where we have excellent reserved positions.

Then the excitement turns to misery.

The front passenger-side tire is flat. I put gloriously-gowned Irene in the front seat, secure the buttons on my rented tuxedo, and spring open the trunk. I wrestle out the dirty spare tire, roll it in position, and then discover that the lug-bolt on the flat tire is stripped.

Now it is 12:30 a.m., and there is no help in sight. Cell phones don't exist yet. The Kennedy Center, almost a mile away, is now locked. President Nixon, Billy Graham, Charlton Heston, Van Cliburn, Pearl Bailey, Joe Lewis (former world heavy weight champion boxer) and all the other famous people we had just been with fade from my mind. All I can see is that flat tire. All I can feel is the icy night, and concern for my beautiful wife shivering in the car in her spectacular evening gown.

Finally a policeman arrives to inquire why we are not leaving the lot. It is almost 1 a.m. He tries to remove the stubborn lug-bolt. It won't yield. At last he radios for a tow truck. It arrives about 1:30 a.m. Irene and I tell the driver we will remain in our car as he hauls us to the all-night service station in Georgetown. The city code will not permit it, so she in her evening gown and I in my fancy tuxedo climb up into the cab and ride the short distance to Georgetown.

By 2 a.m. we are in the service station. It is greasy and dirty. I look at our fancy apparel and suddenly realize how inappropriately dressed we are. Wrong clothes for this place!

Fancy clothes aren't allowed

Multitudes believe they can enter Heaven inappropriately dressed. They have done all possible to bedeck their flesh with the finest, fanciest clothing they can buy. No matter how we garb it, sinful flesh is still sinful flesh. In Heaven, such fancy clothes aren't allowed. Arrogant King Herod put on his flashy royal robes one day, but they provided only a façade, cloaking what was really inside—worms eating their way through his gut. In what had to have been one of the most awkward episodes of history the crawlers nibble through a vital organ, and the king dies ignominiously in front of a group of fawning subjects.

And he no doubt fouls his fancy clothes in the process.

Flesh is like that—no matter how dazzlingly it is covered. In Heaven, the only covering that matters is Christ's. So your first step in Heaven will be out of the old garments of flesh and into the glorious new white robe of the innocence of the Lord Jesus Christ, symbolizing the pristine body in which all people in Christ will be clothed. John, in his vision of Heaven, writes that circling God's Throne "were twenty-four thrones; and upon the thrones I saw twenty-four elders sitting, clothed in white garments, and golden crowns on their heads." (Revelation 4:4)

Later, John says, "I looked, and behold, a great multitude which no one could count, from every nation and all tribes and peoples and tongues, standing before the throne and before the Lamb, clothed in white robes..." (Revelation 7:9)

Here on earth, many are enchanted with their physical bodies. Those who aren't try to make their flesh impressive. In the new earth people will someday flock to the "hill of the Lord" but in our culture we herd ourselves into gymnasia, cosmetic surgeons' offices, and beauty spas. So we must consider why the earthly garment of flesh celebrities celebrate, paparazzi chase, and multitudes admire is not appropriate clothing for Heaven.

Right up front, let's make it clear that the Bible is not anti-(human) body! Some of the old philosophies, like forms of Gnosticism, saw the body as evil at worst, or less good at best. In fact material creation was so inferior to Gnostics that the "high deity" was much too good to have created it. Instead, the physical world was hacked out by lower "gods."

That's definitely not biblical doctrine. God saw *all* that He had made, and behold, it was very good," says Genesis 1:31. And far from being inferior and evil, the human body is the very temple of the Holy Spirit, says 1 Corinthians 6:19. Thus the Holy Spirit is careful to distinguish between "body" and "flesh" with two different Greek words—*soma* for "body" and *sarx* for "flesh." In this world we have a *sarx*-clothed body, but in Heaven we will have a *Christ*-clothed body. A body, yes; *sarx*, No!

Sarx as used in the New Testament refers to the *kronos*-trapped, transitory nature of flesh-life (*bios*). Because of sin, the "default" of the world is downward, from higher to lower quality of life and living. "Flesh"—*sarx*—is to the plunging pull of sin what iron is to a magnet. This is illustrated graphically in the Garden of Eden, when Jesus, after blood-letting agony in prayer, finds His disciples asleep, and says, "you men could not keep watch with Me for one hour?"

Sarx is what makes *soma* vulnerable and transitory. Therefore, the "flesh" has to go because "those who are in the flesh cannot please God." (Romans 8:8)

Maybe you've had one of those chaotic nightmares when you show up before the Queen of England, President of the United States or some other dignitary in your rattiest clothes. Exposure and humiliation are dreadful for most of us. Solomon said God has put eternity in our hearts, the core of our being, and maybe this fear of inappropriate—or insufficient—dress arises from that sense of eternity within us. Maybe our unconscious self knows there is a day when we will appear before the Throne of God, and how terrifying that would be if we were inappropriately dressed, or even naked! The Holy Spirit tells us through Paul in Romans 8:13 that "if you are living according to the flesh, you must die."

Here are some reasons why the "body of this flesh" (Colossians 2:11) is not the right clothing for Heaven:

1. It is not 'fireproof'.

Occasionally while working at the White House I would watch the presidential helicopter land on the South Lawn to ferry the President to Andrews Air Force base or some other location around Washington. Always the Washington DC Fire Department truck would pull onto the lawn. Firefighters in fire-proof suits would be on standby. If the helicopter crashed on landing or takeoff, they were to rush into the flames and rescue the President.

"Our God is a consuming fire," says Hebrews 12:29. God's absolute holiness and perfect purity constitute the blend producing His radiant glory. To go into the Fire of Heaven inappropriately dressed is impossible. This is why we must be "clothed" in Christ, Who is the Second Person in the Godhead, and hence perfectly holy, and therefore "fireproof."

2. The flesh-garment is too stained to be the appropriate clothing for Heaven.

As a young man I worked for a major airline, helping to unload, load and fuel big jets. There came a point when it was futile to wash a uniform. The grease-stains, murk from jet-fuel, smudges from freight and luggage were too deep. The old clothes became rags, and finally had to be tossed out.

Sin-stained flesh is like that. It's beyond redemption. It cannot be cleansed. Isaiah speaks of our fleshly works as "filthy rags." (Isaiah 64:6) It must be "put off"—which means crucified. "Flesh and blood cannot inherit the Kingdom of God," says Paul. (1 Corinthians 15:50) So "those who belong to Christ Jesus have crucified the flesh with its passions and desires." (Galatians 5:24)

3. Flesh is 'selfie'-focused.

"Selfies" are those self-portraits we snap with our cell phones or other digital devices. Other people may be in the picture, but there's no question about who's in focus. Snapchat, Instagram, and other websites make it possible for people to show their faces—and other parts of their anatomy—globally. Since Snapchat alone processes some 350 million selfies daily, it's obvious many people have mostly themselves in mind.[21]

Not surprisingly, "those who are according to the flesh set their minds on the things of the flesh," says Romans 8:5. Tragically, "the mind set on the flesh is death" and "is hostile toward God. (Romans 8:6-7)

The focus in Heaven is God in His fullness, as John sees in the Revelation visions:

> Then I looked, and I heard the voice of many angels around the throne and the living creatures and the elders; and the number of them was myriads of myriads, and thousands of thousands, saying with a loud voice,

---

[21] "My Selfie, Myself," By Jenna Wortham, *The New York Times,* October 19, 2013.

> *"Worthy is the Lamb that was slain to receive power and riches and wisdom and might and honor and glory and blessing." And every created thing which is in heaven and on the earth and under the earth and on the sea, and all things in them, I heard saying, "To Him who sits on the throne, and to the Lamb, be blessing and honor and glory and dominion forever and ever."*
>
> *And the four living creatures kept saying, "Amen." And the elders fell down and worshiped. (Revelation 5:11-14)*

This is no place for "selfie" garments!

4. ***Flesh will deteriorate and therefore cannot endure eternally.***

Sad photos of decaying Detroit are littered over the Internet as I write. One whole collection shows trashed once-elegant neighborhood libraries, wrecked old churches whose mahogany pulpits once thundered with preaching, art deco theaters rotting away, abandoned factories that once made Detroit a thriving city economically, and caved-in mansions.

In a way, decaying cities remind me of what happens to our own physical structures as we age. "My days are like a lengthened shadow, and I wither away like grass," laments the Psalmist. (Psalm 102:11) Solomon is no cheerier when he moans, "All came from the dust and all return to the dust." (Ecclesiastes 3:20) Paul puts it bluntly, in 1 Corinthians 15:50, where he writes, "flesh and blood cannot inherit the kingdom of God; nor does the perishable inherit the imperishable."

In my 70s, I exercise almost every day, watch my diet, and chunk down a basketful of supplements. I feel great, and yet I know I cannot stop, but can only slow the effects of aging. My body is caught in *kronos*, and is not fit for *kairos*. That's why I will need a new one if I am to live in Heaven—and so will you.

In short, flesh cannot be the clothing for Heaven because:

- It is *alien* to the atmosphere of Heaven as a human is alien to the atmosphere of the Marianas Trench, the deepest part of the ocean.
- It is *estranged* from the atmosphere of Heaven as a serial murderer is estranged from Mother Teresa, who spent a lifetime caring for the Calcutta dying in Jesus' Name.
- It is physically *contradictory* to the physics of Heaven as antimatter is to matter.

To say that "flesh" (sarx) cannot inhabit Heaven is not to say that we will be without a body. "If there is a natural body, there is also a spiritual body," says 1 Corinthians 44. Further, says Paul, "we know that if the earthly tent which is our house is torn down, we have a building from God, a house not made with hands, eternal in the heavens." (2 Corinthians 5:1)

Two Big Questions

1. ***What will this body be like?***

What the Bible reveals about the resurrection body of Jesus Christ, plus the revelations of other scriptural passages give us some insights about what our bodies will be like in Heaven.

- **Enhanced senses**

Heaven is a wonder-world for the senses. We will have our five senses—and probably more—but at levels we cannot imagine. They fall somewhere in that category Paul has in mind through the Holy Spirit when he writes, in 1 Corinthians 2:9,

> "No eye has seen, no ear has heard,
> and no mind has imagined
> what God has prepared
> for those who love him." NLT

Our eyes will see color with unimaginable beauty. I am an autumn guy, and toward October I yearn to see the color in the backyard of Appalachia where I was born and raised. I know the desire in my soul is the eternity in my heart, and the anticipation of what I *will* see in Heaven. Our ears will hear music that floods the soul with the glory of its harmonies. To me perhaps the most beautiful chord in all music occurs in *Nessun Dorma,* the magnificent aria in Puccini's opera, *Turandot.* The chord is a flourish, arising in the wake of the stunning voice of a tenor like Luciano Pavarotti. Sometimes I get tears over its loveliness. I cannot imagine anything more soul-satisfying, and yet in Heaven my new ears will hear even more beautiful sounds. Our noses will take in the aroma of heavenly incense. Our hands will clutch the palm branches that we will wave before the Lord of Glory. Our taste will experience the rich feast at the banquet table of the Bride.

Nothing on earth can come close. Peter, James, and John had a small tidbit of the heavenly experience on the Mount of Transfiguration. They didn't want to come down, and I am sure that none of our loved ones now in Heaven would want to leave. Nor will we!

When I think of earthly beauty, my mind journeys to Kerala, the southernmost state of India. I made the first of several trips to India in 1971. My first destination there was Kerala. The trip had been wearying, but the experiences there awakened all my senses. I had never seen a sky so blue. The green of hardy palms danced across the canvas of the cerulean sky. At ground level my eyes feasted on varieties of flowers and their luxuriant colors. People were arrayed in multi-hued saris. The sounds were equally wonderful—the musical language, the chatter of animals, the splashing of the sea. The smells were lavish with spices, the tastes remarkable, and the feel of the place has lingered in my soul all these years.

And yet it was not perfect. Kerala, like Texas and everywhere else in the world still lies as it did then under the curse of human sin, whose radiating effect scorches all we touch and are part of, all the way up to the universe itself, as Romans 8 tells us. Disease, decay, exploitation, poverty, abuse were and are all there in lovely Kerala.

How remarkable it will be in living in and traveling through curse-free Heaven in a curse-free body! We know these Heaven-qualified bodies will have senses: there will be the Glory of God to see, heavenly music to hear with orchestras and voices singing a "new song", fragrant incense to smell, delectable food to eat, and many tangible things pleasant to the touch.

- **Unlimited mobility**

There is a sense in which our fears are the reverse images of the freedom and joy of Heaven.

One of the most heroic people in our church is Frank Andrews. Some of us remember many years ago when Frank, with assistance and courage, hobbled up to the platform in our worship center to give his testimony. He told us that he had been diagnosed with Lou Gehrig disease, and that he wouldn't be able to walk much longer as atrophy gradually immobilized his muscles.

With great sorrow we watched Frank lose his power of movement. But Frank would not be conquered. He turned his own immobility into a ministry. Frank's technologically brilliant mind was not immobilized, and he invented computer devices to help people immobilized like himself. You can still see Frank almost every Sunday, sitting in a big wheelchair right at the back of our church.

We admire Frank's courage because most of us have a terror of being closed in, trapped. This is because eternity is in our hearts, and the greatest physical freedom we will experience is in Heaven. Neither time nor space will be able to imprison us. Yes, there are walls in the New Jerusalem, says the Bible, but not walls to keep us penned up, but only to symbolize that there is a horrible "outside", called Hell, which can never break into Heaven!

Jesus gave us a preview of the absolute mobility of the heavenly body when, after His resurrection, He kept appearing before His followers. If they were in a little room in a small mud house, He could move through the walls. If they went up to Galilee to try to fish and forget their sorrows, He could be manifest in Galilee with them. He transcended the tangible world, yet could touch—gathering fire sticks, catching fish, and broiling them for His still-earthly friends.

- **Inexhaustible energy**

There are four big reasons you will experience inexhaustible energy in your heavenly body. First, you will have *Zoe* as the totality of your life, with no mixture of *bios*, the existent, functional life in the natural world. Second, you will inhabit a form of time that does not move from past to future, and hence there is no "time" for you to wear out. Third, you are "clothed" in an "imperishable" body. Fourth, you breathe in the wonderful air of Heaven, free of carcinogens, allergens, and all the other pollutants that corrupt our health.

Back on earth, this may explain the vast ages to which people lived in the primeval world. Prior to sin, their bodies were of heavenly quality, with the added ability to exist in the natural world. But since that world had not yet been corrupted by sin, it was pristine and pure. Once sin enters it is like cancer, and will advance until something stops it. The body increasingly is affected by the advance of sin, and so is the world itself. Over time, the human gene pool deteriorates, and lifespans shorten.

But in that dawning age before evil corrupted everything, the world's inhabitants had inexhaustible energy. Adam tended the garden, but that work didn't become "labor" until sin entered (Genesis 3: 17-19)

Entropy is the dissipation of energy and a breakdown of order over time. But entropy is one of those natural phenomena that, as the Psalmist put it, testifies to the glory of God, and that, as Paul wrote in Romans 1, give witness to God's reality. Deterioration is movement from a higher order to a lower. Therefore, entropy infers that there was once an absolute steady-state of energy and order from which there has been a decline.

Peter, the unschooled fisherman, in his second sermon after the Pentecost event, said something so profound that not even he knew the full extent of what he was saying. Jesus will not come until kronos-time has arrived at the climactic junction with kairos-time, which will be the moment for "the restitution of all things." (Acts 3:21)

That means the heavenly world is and will be returned to the state of inexhaustible energy when nothing wears out—including that new body you will inhabit.

2. When will we receive the new body?

The answer is both *immediately* upon our death passage, and also in the *future*.

How can this be in light of what Paul wrote about the sequential order of resurrection. Here are two passages where he talks about sequence:

- **1 Corinthians 15:20-25**

But now Christ has been raised from the dead, the first fruits of those who are asleep. For since by a man came death, by a man also came the resurrection of the dead. For as in Adam all die, so also in Christ all will be made alive. But each in his own order: Christ the first fruits, after that those who are Christ's at His coming, then comes the end, when He hands over the kingdom to the God and Father, when He has abolished all rule and all authority and power.

- **1 Thessalonians 4:13-17**

But we do not want you to be uninformed, brethren, about those who are asleep, so that you will not grieve as do the rest who have no hope. For if we believe that Jesus died and rose again, even so God will bring with Him those who have fallen asleep in Jesus. For this we say to you by the word of the Lord, that we who are alive and remain until the coming of the Lord, will not precede those who have fallen asleep. For the Lord Himself will descend from heaven with a shout, with the voice of the archangel and with the trumpet of God, and the dead in Christ will rise first. Then we who are alive and remain will be caught up together with them in the clouds to meet the Lord in the air, and so we shall always be with the Lord.

Paul says the truth about our dying and receiving our new bodies is a "mystery." It seems to be a riddle. However, a clue to the mystery is found in the Greek of the New Testament.

Remember, two levels of time are interacting here—kronos (earth-time) and kairos (Heaven-time). From the kronos-perspective of having new bodies that will be able to live in the "new heavens and the new earth" we must wait, since it is in the kronos (chronological) future. But when we die we step immediately into kairos, where there is no sequential limitation on time. Thus 1 Corinthians 15 speaks primarily from the kronos perspective, but we will also be clothed "immediately" with the imperishable body since when we step out of earth-time, we step into Heaven-time where there is no "waiting" for the future. Heaven-time is tenseless: no past or future, only the Continuum.

"If there is a natural body, there is also a spiritual body," writes the Apostle Paul. (1 Corinthians 15:44-45) And he ought to know, because Paul had been given a rare pre-death glimpse of the Third Heaven—the Highest Heaven. (2 Corinthians 12:1-6)

Death is therefore a "stepping out" of the body of flesh and "stepping in" to the body of Heaven—the Resurrection Body of Jesus the Christ.

That leads to another critical question: Is this new body an empty shell? Paul spoke of the body as a "tent", and the purpose of a tent is to provide shelter for something or someone.

When you step out of your old body you leave behind the old soul with its stinging memories, turbulent emotions, and rebellious will. When you step into your new body you discover it comes with the whole internal "package"—not divided spirit *and* soul, but united spirit-soul!

Chapter 5

STEPPING OUT, STEPPING IN

The New Soul

Your first step in Heaven will be into your new body, *and* into your new soul. The heavenly body will be your clothing, but you will not be an "empty suit".

Contemporary culture has given us many sarcastic and satirical expressions. For example, if you know someone who is a fake, who makes no real contribution to anything, has no accomplishments, and is a waste of everyone's time he is often referred to as an "empty suit".

That would describe one of my favorite literary characters. Bertie Wooster, an empty-headed, empty-hearted, and thus an "empty suit" was created by 20th century British novelist P.G. Wodehouse. Wooster is a 1930s English aristocrat whose inheritance makes it possible for him to have a butler named Jeeves, a fancy apartment in the posh London Mayfair neighborhood, and membership in an elite old-boys club where he hangs out daily.

At one point a person tells Wooster that she has heard about all his great accomplishments. Actually, someone else trying to make Wooster look good had misrepresented him to the woman. Wooster mutters to himself: *Accomplishments?*

I can't remember having any accomplishments. He turns to Jeeves for help. "Jeeves, have I accomplished anything?"

For that reason and many more in Wodehouse's hilarious *Jeeves and Wooster* series there could not be a better illustration of an "empty suit" than Bertie Wooster.

In contrast to Wooster and all the non-fictional people he so graphically exemplifies, David Aikman writes about real people he calls "Great Souls". He details six of them and their contributions to society summed up in one word:

Billy Graham: Salvation
Nelson Mandela: Forgiveness
Aleksandr Solzhenitsyn: Truth
Mother Teresa: Compassion
Pope John Paul II: Human Dignity
Elie Wiesel: Remembrance[22]

The secret behind the immense impact of these men and women was in the greatness of their souls, says Aikman. Character qualities reside in the soul, he suggests. Aikman believes the soul is a person's "total self in its living unity and wholeness... man's moral and emotional nature as distinguished from his mind or intellect."

Aikman writes this about the six "Great Souls" he examines in his book:

---

[22] David Aikman, *Great Souls,* Nashville: Word Publishing, XIII.

What was it about Mother Teresa that caught the imagination of the whole world? Or about Solzhenitsyn that seemed to provide the catalyst for the demolition of Marxist-Leninist Utopianism as a plausible future for the human race? Or about Elie Wiesel that forces us, again and again, to address the profundity of evil of which the human race, under the Nazis, showed itself so capable? Or about Billy Graham that has made the salvation of the human soul an issue of extraordinary urgency across the world for five decades? Or about Nelson Mandela that turned his most intransigent adversaries—even his jailers—into supporters of his particular social and political visions? Or about Pope John Paul II that has saved the papacy from becoming just an emblem of archaic spirituality, instead transforming it into a vital debating chair for global issues that are entirely contemporary?

Aikman says what made all these contributions possible was the virtue of character of these men and women, residing in their souls.

'Meeting point of spirit and body'

Watchman Nee, the great Chinese follower of Jesus Christ, also wrote about the soul. Aikman, himself a committed disciple of Jesus, wrote about greatness of soul, but Nee examines the flaws as well as the goodness. In a sweeping study of all the Bible's teachings about the soul, Nee concludes it "is the natural life" of a human being, "the power that makes us alive in the flesh... that "animates every member" of our bodies.[23] The soul, he finds, is the "meeting point" of spirit and body. Nee shows that functionally the Bible reveals that the human soul is the organ of thinking, feeling, and choosing—mind, emotions, and will. Therefore, we will not be "empty suits" in Heaven, but all of us will have truly "great souls" because they will be of a new quality.

In the last study we saw that we will have new bodies with all the senses present and vastly enhanced. So we will have new souls with thinking that functions fully with the Mind of Christ, emotions that know the unlimited peace and joy of the Spirit, and wills that choose only what God the Father chooses. All this means freedom from the torment of bad memories, freedom from chaotic emotions, and freedom from the guilt and disasters that come from wrong choices.

As my wife reminded me, in light of the differences of quality in the time-dimensions of kronos and kairos, we already have our new bodies and new souls. In kronos-time we have not yet stepped into them, but they are there in Heaven, like a magnificent garment stored in a safe and secure vault, waiting for us to step inside and put them on.

---

[23] Watchman Nee, *The Spiritual Man, Volume I,* New York: Christian Fellowship Publishers, 142.

There are many who either don't know or reject the Bible's teaching about the destiny of the soul. They acknowledge that there is some inner dynamic that provides all the functions we relate to soul. But if Heaven is not real according to these philosophies, where does the soul go when we die? There are several theories:

- *Christoplatonism,* the idealism of Plato embraced by many Christians, holds that the body is merely a shell that the soul leaves behind at death, like a snake sheds an old skin. The soul lives in Heaven in a disembodied state.
- *Reincarnation* is the belief that a soul leaves the body at death and is reborn in a different human.
- *Transmigration* teaches that the soul leaves the body at death, and may take up residence in humans or animals, and is part of the purification that brings us finally to return "home" to cosmic consciousness or reunion with the "One."

None of these is found in the Bible. The soul does not exist in a disembodied state in Heaven. It does not leap from human to human. It does not cross over species lines into animals. The good news that is the Gospel is that Christ saves us wholly, spirit, soul, and body, and our first step in Heaven is the step into the wholeness of spirit, soul, and body God intended for us from the very beginning!

To appreciate the new soul in Heaven we must understand the soul we have in earth. Someone has said that the human being, made in the image of God, is a spirit-being inhabiting a body, and possessing a soul. Humanity got a body when God shaped Adam from the dust of the ground. But when did we get a soul?

A brief history of the soul

Genesis 2:7 reveals that after God formed the physical structure of the human being, He "breathed" into its nostrils, and the form "became a living soul." In that moment there was a union of *bios*—the existent type of life, and *Zoe*, the being-essence of life. As I noted in previous chapters, *bios* is the quantitative aspect of the human, enabling existence in material form within kronos-time and finite space. *Zoe* is the qualitative dimension of the human, initially linked directly to Heaven. *Zoe* was and is the very life-quality of God. The human body is made as its Temple, as Paul writes in 1 Corinthians 6:19.

As the *Zoe*-essence floods into *bios*-existence the man becomes a "living *nephesh*," in the Hebrew of Genesis 2:7. The Hebrew term is essential for proper understanding of the soul in God's original, pristine design and creation. The King James Version accurately renders it "soul" because of all the meanings embedded in the word: emotion, thought, volition, personality, character, self-awareness to name a few.

The key is in the fact that God *breathed* into the form the "breath of life." "Breath in Hebrew is *ruach*. The corresponding word in New Testament Greek is *pneuma*, which is translated as "spirit". The soul animates the body but the Spirit of God animates the soul. Randy Alcorn writes that

> "The point at which Adam became *nephesh* is when God joined his body (dust) and spirit (breath) together. Adam was not a living human being until he had both material (physical) and immaterial (spiritual) components. Thus, the essence of humanity is not just spirit, but *spirit joined with body.*"[24]

We cannot understand the soul without the spirit any more than we can grasp the meaning of a hydroelectric turbine without water. Atheistic Darwinists like Richard Dawkins work hard to try to make the human over again, not in the image of God, but in the image of animals. But they cannot get rid of the unique design of the human, who consists of spirit, soul, and body. (1 Thessalonians 5:23). The spirit is the pesky component of the human that simply will not go away. Because it is intended in God's design as the organ that can establish linkage with Him, making communion with the Transcendent possible, the presence of the spirit shows that the human being is distinct from the animals.

There are at least two ways the atheists try to get around this. One is to deny the reality of the human spirit. There is no "spirit", they say, just an illusionary idea foisted

---

[24] Randy Alcorn, *Heaven,* Tyndale House Publishers, 112.

on us by evolution's drive for survivability. The other way atheists try to get rid of the idea of the human spirit is by lowering the ceiling of transcendence.

London comedians Sanderson Jones and Pippa Evans founded The Sunday Assembly, an atheist "church", or "godless congregation."[25] Their church is "dedicated to acts of benevolence and the search for transcendence." However, they reveal that when atheists start looking for transcendence they set the ceiling too low. "Transcendence," Jones and Evans declare, "can be found in a breath of wind on your face or in a mouthful of custard tart."

Refreshing winds and luscious custards cannot be truly transcendent because they are not Wholly Other. Leonard Krishtalka of the University of Kansas once described Intelligent Design as "nothing more than creationism in a cheap tuxedo." But I would term Jones' and Evans' "godless" transcendence as nothing more than immanence on stilts.

Max Planck, "the patriarch of Quantum Theory,"[26] faced honestly the dilemma of the finite immanent when he wrote, "over the gates of the temple of science are written the words: Ye must have faith... Science cannot solve the ultimate mystery of nature... because in the last analysis, we ourselves are a part of nature and therefore a part of the very mystery that we are trying to solve."

---

[25] "Do Atheists Exist?" By Nicholas Frankovich, *National Review Online*, December 28, 2013.
[26] "Bo Jinn", *Illogical Atheism*.

Saint Paul was speaking of liberation from the finite immanent when he said, "I press on toward the goal for the prize of the upward call of God in Christ Jesus." (Philippians 3:14) Isaiah experienced that life-transforming, destiny-setting freedom when he saw God "high and lifted up." (Isaiah 6) The most bracing of winds and the most delectable custard tarts don't seem to have that kind of lifting power. This is important because we are qualitatively lifted up or reduced to the level of that which we worship.

So in God's original design there were to be no barriers between spirit and soul. Each would have its own functions, but the operations would be interconnected. Mind, emotion, and will, all functions of the soul, could not work properly if not empowered and guided by the spirit. And the human spirit could not perform correctly if it was not indwelt and empowered by God's Holy Spirit. In turn, the body would receive and implement the thoughts, feelings, and choices of the soul, conceived and driven by the spirit that receives the direct commands and empowerment of the Holy Spirit. This leads to superlative human "performance," personal wholeness and health, qualitatively as well as quantitatively

Therefore, *the original, mint condition of the human being is spirit-soul, a union that constitutes the inner being housed in the body.*

Among the greatest tragedies of sin is that it splits spirit and soul, and thereby fragments the human being. This results in the condition Paul describes in Galatians 5:17:

> The old sinful nature loves to do evil, which is just opposite from what the Holy Spirit wants. And the Spirit gives us desires that are opposite from what the sinful nature desires. These two forces are constantly fighting each other, and your choices are never free from this conflict. (NLT)

The outcomes range from psychological dysfunction and moral breakdown to the destruction of physical health as stresses and lifestyle practices are cut off by the soul from the influence of the Holy Spirit upon the human spirit.

'Men without chests'

"We make men without chests and expect from them virtue and enterprise," wrote C.S. Lewis in one of his insightful books, *The Abolition of Man*. The "chest" is the repository of the "heart", used often in the Bible to signify the innermost being of the human—the spirit. Lewis' profound point is that when the spirit is dead because of the absence of the Holy Spirit (having been rejected) our ideal humanity is "abolished". Despite the Darwinists, being just another animal is not something to celebrate, for it infers the loss of the Imago Dei, the image of God. This is why Romans 3:23 describes sin as "falling short" of God's glory, His Image. When we behave like animals we are not being truly human because we are not functioning in the Spirit of God.

But one of the most beautiful scenes in the great epic of Jesus Christ is found in John 20:22. The risen Jesus encounters His followers, and "He breathed on them and said to them, 'Receive the Holy Spirit.'"

Don't lose this powerful moment: It is a re-institution of what happened in Genesis 2:7 when God breathed into Adam's nostrils and the clump of clay became a "living *nephesh*", a spirit-soul living being. The Zoe-giving Spirit is now infused back into the human spirit that has been empty so long. All who receive Christ receive His Spirit, and the Holy of Holies of the temple of their being is no longer vacant. (Romans 8:1-11) This is why Holy Spirit-indwelt people are "new creations in Christ Jesus." (2 Corinthians 5:17)

Therefore when the person redeemed and renewed by Jesus Christ and indwelt by the Holy Spirit dies, he or she is immediately in the new body that contains the new spirit-soul. Let's consider what this means for each part of the soul.

- **The Mind**

Immediately when we receive Jesus Christ as our Savior the Holy Spirit enters our human spirit with the fullness of Christ. Jesus describes what happens when He says the Holy Spirit will

> "take of (receive, draw upon) what is Mine and will reveal (declare, disclose, transmit) it to you. Everything that the Father has is Mine. That is what I meant when I said that He [the Spirit] will take the things that are Mine and

will reveal (declare, disclose, transmit) it to you." (John 16:14-15 Amplified Bible)

Therefore, as Paul writes, "we *have* the mind of Christ." (1 Corinthians 2:16) The being we already are and that is already "seated with Christ in heavenly places" (Ephesians 2:6) has the mind of Christ. Thus when we die, "we shall know as we are known" because we will know everything Christ knows.

But if we already have the Mind of Christ why don't we "know" now? The answer is in those experiences we've all had in which something obscures our view. The first time I flew to Los Angeles was on a red-eye flight that landed in the wee hours. On the approach I could see the array of lights below but nothing else. My business kept me in the Los Angeles area for three days. On the afternoon of the third, I took off for home. I was amazed as the airplane climbed to see that mountains ring the great city. I had been right at their base for almost three whole days and never once seen them. The reason: smog.

The Mind of Christ is embedded in our spirit through the Holy Spirit. As I pointed out above, the New Testament Greek term for "spirit" is *pneuma*. "Pneumatic" is a derivative of this word. It speaks of energy, the force of a gale. Christ's powerful thought and intellect emerge in our souls as the Spirit blows away the smog. The filling of the Holy Spirit is a lifelong process by which more and more of our faculties of mind, emotion, and will are "set apart" (sanctified) for Christ and His use.

The Holy Spirit reveals to Paul, and through him, to us, what happens when the Holy Spirit drives away the obscuring gloom. We not only begin to see what was hidden in the murk, but we see everything from a different perspective. As we experience the Mind of Christ, says Paul, we can appraise and evaluate every phenomenon, every experience, every movement, every theory from God's infinite perspective rather than from our earth-based conceptualizations. (1 Corinthians 2:10-16)

What kind of memories will we have in Heaven? Will we remember the bad and hurtful things? Since we will have the omniscience of Christ's Mind, our memories cannot be less than what they were in the earth and kronos-time. However, what we remember of those events is the presence of God and His providence through and in them. We will remember them with delight because of the way we look at the "diamond" of experience and thought.

A very limited illustration: I remember a set of "bad decisions" made almost 50 years ago that interrupted by career path. But now I can see those choices from the perspective of age 72. God did not select those "bad decisions" for me, but gave me the freedom to make the choices. However, God used the decisions to build a different kind of career than what I had imagined, one that would open doors and take me places I could not reach or even know existed. So from my view higher up the "mountain" of kronos, memories that once gave me immense pain are now happy. I don't have the lesser perspective but a greater understanding because the memories are still there, but now amplified by the Holy Spirit's illumination. I see the hand of God in the mess I made, and the mess is now seen as His instrument.

God will do that with all your memories because in Heaven you have spirit-soul!

Further, think of the range of knowledge regarding the deepest mysteries of the universe. As we discussed earlier, Francis Collins, a medical doctor and biochemist received a huge assignment from the United States government. His mission was to lead the Human Genome Project, by his own description, an "audacious effort to read the entire sequence of all the human DNA." He and his team achieved their goal, and opened new vistas of understanding for treating and curing disease.

Dr. Collins says he had been a "pretty obnoxious atheist" in the early twenties, but after serious consideration of the plausibility of biblical faith, and reading C.S. Lewis he became a serious Christian at age 27. He sees no conflict between science and faith. In fact,

> "... as a person of faith, that moment of discovery has an additional dimension. It's appreciating something, realizing something, knowing something that up until then no human had known - but God knew it. And there is an intricacy and elegance in the nature of biology, particularly when it comes to the information carrying capacity of DNA, which is rather awesome. And so, in a way, perhaps,

> those moments of discovery also become moments of worship, moments of appreciation, of the incredible intricacies and beauty of biology, of the world, of life. And, therefore, an appreciation of God as the creator."[27]

The wonder of Heaven is that the mind, free from the obscuring smog of sin and its consequences in the fallen world, will have that "moment of discovery" immediately. All the beauty of God's creation known to Francis Collins and other great thinkers will be known to the person who died as a child, or unschooled adult. In fact, the heavenly mind will know more than Collins or Einstein or Dawkins knew on earth because the new mind will know and experience all the omniscience of God Himself through the Mind of Christ.

- **The Emotions**

Human emotions are the seismograph of the mind. They register every tremor and spike at every quake. The mind takes in information, processes it against the backdrop of the fallen soul without the guidance and restraint of the Spirit, and floods the emotions like an explosive tsunami.

The human soul craves the emotions of peace and joy like the body craves food and water. Yet few of us really know what real peace and joy are. In our fallen body and soul-driven lives we confuse avoidance or compromise for peace and pleasure or happiness for joy. We do experience

---

[27] "Faith and Reason: An Interview With Francis Collins, http://www.pbs.org/faithandreason/transcript/coll-body.html.

those rare moments when a little bit of Heaven breaks into our lives. "Heaven will be the answer to every prayer, every desire for healing, physical, emotional, mental, and spiritual," writes Peter Kreeft. "All healings on earth are previews of coming attractions."[28]

The Bible gives us tantalizing clues regarding the critical emotions of joy and peace. "In Your presence is fullness of joy... in Your right hand are pleasures forever," says Psalm 16:11.

There are two levels of the "presence" of God. First, is the *objective* presence. Jesus will never forsake us, but is with us always, whether we experience His presence or not. (Matthew 28:20; Hebrews 13:5) This is the *promise* of the presence. This is objective fact, whether there is subjective experience or not. I don't necessarily "feel" the presence of God driving on Houston's bolting freeways, but He is present because He said He would be.

Second is the manifest, or *subjective* presence of God. If the objective presence is the *promise* of the presence, the manifest, subjective presence is the *presence* of the promise. This is the breakthrough of heavenly atmospherics into our life situation in this world. David was hungering for the restoration of this presence and its subjective manifestation when he cried, "restore to me the joy of Your salvation!" (Psalm 51:12)

Most of us would likely say that the promise of the presence is what we rely on mostly in this world. This is

---

[28] Peter Kreeft, *Everything You Ever Wanted to Know About Heaven.*

consistent with the walk of faith, which strengthens so many suffering people. That's why the manifest presence is a breakthrough. However, in the new emotions of the new soul in Heaven the manifest, subjective presence will be the only experience, and therefore we will have fullness of joy. "Fullness" means there will be nothing to dilute it, and nothing to cut it short because we will never leave the subjective experience of the presence of God!

The same will be true of the peace our new souls will have as a continual state. In the Revelation vision John sees that because Heaven's inhabitants dwell continually with God without the corroding of the curse or the terminating effect of kronos-time, "He will wipe away every tear from their eyes." Further, "there will no longer be any mourning, or crying, or pain." (Revelation 21:1-4)

This is because of the spatial and temporal nature of Heaven. First, "there is no longer any sea." (Revelation 21:1) That is, there are no spatial dividers in Heaven that cut people off from God and one another. Second, "there will be no longer any death." (Revelation 21:4) Because we will dwell in kairos rather than kronos, time will not cut us off from our beloved ones.

The result will be joy and peace without limitations. Our spirit-soul in Heaven will no longer be a chunk of concrete pulling us down into despair, hopelessness, fear, and confusion, but our spirit-soul will be as wings, lifting us up into the ecstasy of the manifest presence of God!

The Will

The third function of the soul is volition. The soul, therefore, is the seat of the will. We have a will because we are not robots, but God's image bearers: God wills, therefore we will. Will infers freedom, for if there were no freedom the capacity to will would be as useless as ship without water or an airplane without air.

We make our choices in this world, but the ultimate effects are received and experienced in Heaven. We certainly experience consequences of our decisions in the here-and-now, but destiny-determining outcomes are given to us in Heaven.

This is the meaning of judgment. For example, people who in this world exercise their will to reject God's invitation to salvation will hear only one thing when they die: "I never knew you; depart from Me." (Matthew 7:23) This will be spoken with great sadness because the Lord "is not willing that any should perish but that all should come to repentance." (2 Peter 3:9)

While those in Christ won't hear those chilling words, their works will be judged. All Spirit-indwelt people receive spiritual gifts to carry out their earthly mission for Christ and His Kingdom. Most of us will at times willfully misapply these gifts or choose to rely entirely on the human "might" and "power" rather than God's Spirit and the gifts He imparts and energizes within and through us. (Zechariah 4:6) Therefore our works will be tested, and only those that have manifested Christ and His Kingdom, and have advanced its cause in the world will endure.

The human will is what gets us all in trouble. Adam and Eve *chose* the forbidden fruit. We are sinners because we have a sin nature, and our sin nature predisposes us to *choose* sin. The fundamental issue with respect to the will is whether it is actually free or under the control of determinism. The question, then, is this: In Heaven is the human will totally free or under the deterministic control of the all-Sovereign God?

The answer is surprising: It is in the natural world, because of sin, that the will is actually much more restricted than in Heaven. In fact, in Heaven, the will is totally free because it is as free as the will of God!

Think of it this way: Every time we seek to follow God more closely our flesh resists. That's because it is the servant of sin, and sin is enslavement. (Ephesians 4:1-11) Therefore, we have limited freedom in the fallen world, not because God has placed the limitations on our freedom, but Satan and sin restrict us by placing us in the prison of the flesh. Please note: this does not mean we are helpless victims. *We* actually give the authority for Satan to enslave us by giving him "ground" or a place to build a stronghold in our lives. (Ephesians 4:17)

We are therefore not really free to choose God and His Kingdom totally and absolutely as long as we place ourselves under the bondage of the flesh.

The relationship between militant atheist Richard Dawkins and his daughter, Juliet, illustrates the problem.

When she was 10, Daddy Dawkins wrote a letter to his daughter about how life works. He warned her about people who would try to impose beliefs on her. Dawkins did not have atheists in mind, but those obnoxious religious believers (he ignores the fact that atheism is a "religious belief"). Here's part of what Dawkins said to 10-year old Juliet:

> Next time somebody tells you something that sounds important, think to yourself: 'Is this the kind of thing that people probably know because of evidence? Or is it the kind of thing that people only believe because of tradition, authority or revelation?' And, next time somebody tells you that something is true, why not say to them: 'What kind of evidence is there for that?' And if they can't give you a good answer, I hope you'll think very carefully before you believe a word they say.

One might infer that Richard Dawkins is at peace with his daughter having enough free will to choose to believe in God, to question the "tradition" of Darwinism and its doctrines that "sound important." She might even be free to ask her father to give her the "evidences" that God does not exist. But that's not likely the case. Juliet therefore has limited free will within the boundaries set by her father.

The Father, however, does not impose boundaries on our freewill because we are completely free to choose our heart's true desire—God.

Note what happens when the human will is aligned with God's will: "Delight yourself in the Lord, and He will give you the desires of your heart," says Psalm 37:4. In Heaven your new soul's total delight is "in the Lord" and therefore He wills to give you that for which your desires will, which conform totally to what He wills.

"There are only two kinds of people in the end," writes C.S. Lewis,

> "those who say to God, 'Thy will be done,' and those to whom God says, 'Thy will be done.' All that are in Hell, choose it. Without that self-choice there could be no Hell. No soul that seriously and constantly desires joy will ever miss it. Those who seek find. To those who knock it is opened."[29]

Friedrich Nietzsche, the 19th century German philosopher, illustrates those who say to God, "*my* will be done," and he thus shows us a bit of Hell-on-earth. "My idea is that every specific body strives to become master over all space and to extend its force (its will to power) and to thrust back all that resists its extension," he said. In his personal life, Nietzsche bumped up against the "resistance" of God,

---

[29] C.S. Lewis, *The Great Divorce*.

and "thrust back", asserting his own will. Nietzsche rejected the very idea of Heaven, believing it hindered human effectiveness in this life. He was so extreme in his resistance to God that Nietzsche ultimately wrote that "God is dead." But in the end it was Nietzsche who was dead from insanity and syphilis.

The new soul in the new body knows no insanity, no neurosis or psychosis because the will in that "new creation" is not in conflict with that of the Almighty, whose will is its perpetual delight. Therefore those secure in Christ have no paranoia, no anxiety, and no fear about standing before the piercing eyes of the Lord Himself!

Chapter 6

STANDING BEFORE THE SEVEN EYES

Your first step into Heaven—the realm so far away that it is beyond our universe and yet as near as the next room in your house—is to step into the new body and new soul, and to stand immediately before the One Whose "eyes are like flaming fire." (Revelation 1:14)

And those eyes are piercing right through you. They read the reality of your earthly life instantly. Nothing is hidden. Nothing is forgotten—except the sins whose guilt has been removed from you as far as the east is from the west because you have confessed them and received God's forgiveness and forgetfulness.

The Scripture leaves no doubt that the first step in Heaven with that new body and soul is to also step into judgment.

Many years ago Irene and I, accompanied by a small team, were headed for Africa on a mission. I was especially excited because one of the team members was a native of the country where we were going to serve. I knew he would be invaluable in his work. He was excited about seeing family and friends back home in Africa.

We arrived at Houston's George Bush Intercontinental Airport and moved quickly to the airline counter for check-in. I watched as my African friend presented his ticket and documents. Suddenly things went wrong. The letter he carried from the American immigration authority was not sufficient to allow him to fly internationally. The man was distraught. Sadly he walked away from the counter. As I passed through security I saw him standing at the terminal exit, waiting for a ride to take him back to his temporary residence in Houston. He was turned away at the gate.

Multitudes of people arrive at the end of their journey on earth with the full expectation that Heaven is their next destination. But they will be dismayed when a quick evaluation shows they cannot enter Heaven. Their shock will be devastating as they are turned away at the "gate".

In a sense, the airline ticket counter was a point of "judgment" where it's determined if a person can board the airplane or not. And even for those who are allowed to fly, there is still a "judgment" regarding what they can bring on board. Trash cans and special containers are all around the security area of an airport, full of items passengers can't carry into the airplane. Piercing scanners look into the core of briefcases, purses, boxes, small carry-on bags, and, through X-Ray, even into our physical bodies, and see all.

Your first step into Heaven is the step into a highly restricted domain. Only those whose names are recorded and known there are admitted. And those who are allowed in have "baggage" that must be eliminated because the contents don't measure up to the richness of the Kingdom of Heaven.

Ironically, every time atheists go to court in pursuit of "justice" they are showing the "eternity in their hearts" and confirming the haunting reality of judgment to come—which they labor hard to suppress. Every courtroom on earth is a testimony for the reality of the Absolute Court of Judgment, for if there is no Absolute Standard there is no measure of rightness-wrongness, legality-illegality. If there is no Absolute Standard there are no grounds for a case pleading justice because anything and everything may be considered "just". Apart from the Absolute, the term is as meaningless as a measuring stick in a world without quantity and number.

The mysterious passion to 'set things right'

Thomas Sowell is one of the most insightful writers of our time. Though he grew up in Harlem and was educated in its schools, he gained entry to Harvard. He is as wise as an Edmund Burke or a G.K. Chesterton—two of my heroes. One of the most illuminating concepts he has given contemporary culture is *The Quest for Cosmic Justice,* the title of one of his books.

Even philosophers and social justice crusaders who deny God and Judgment-to-come are driven by the passion to set things right and achieve fairness or equitability. Though they blame inequality and unfairness on society, Sowell says that some of the them "often recognize that some undeserved inequalities may arise from cultural differences, family genes, or from historical confluences of events not controlled by anybody or by any given society at any given time… Crusaders for social justice seek to correct not merely the sins of man but the oversights of God or the accidents of history… What they are really seeking is a universe tailor-made to their vision of equality. They are seeking cosmic justice."[30]

In other words they have some inkling of ultimate justice and have an expectation that the cosmos set things straight in the end. The "eternity" at the core of the human spirit knows that Ultimate Judgment is coming, when perfect justice will prevail for all.

In fact, the loss of the idea of Judgment and Hell from Western culture has had disastrous consequences. Sowell himself illustrates this. "Thank God my teachers in Harlem were unfair to me when I was growing up," he says. One, Miss Simon, made him write 50 times every word he misspelled. Miss Simon herself was educated in a period when the sense of accountability derived from that larger Accountability coming at the end of life was a theme thundered from the old pulpits that valued truth over therapy. Though Sowell was a high school drop-out, and

---

[30] http://www.tsowell.com/spquestc.html

came from a family in which no one had ever gone to college, and could not afford books, he passed Harvard's formidable entrance exam.

Speaking of Harvard, two of its researchers, Robert Barrio and Rachel McClary studied the relationship between religious belief and a nation's economic prosperity. They concluded that "a belief in Hell was a slightly more potent economic spur than a belief in Heaven."[31] People with a sense of the afterlife also carry an awareness of accountability, producing a higher work ethic and greater productivity.

Externally, the universe is moved by "facts," writes Dinesh D'Souza. But we humans, he observes, "are internally moved by "values" that "defy natural and scientific laws." These internal values "contradict the powerful engine of human self-interest, giving morality an undeniable anti-evolutionary thrust." The explanation, thinks D'Souza, lies in the "presupposition of cosmic justice, achieved not in this life but in another life beyond the grave." This, he believes, explains "why humans continue to espouse goodness and justice even when the world is evil and unjust."[32]

The shadow of Judgment Day doesn't just haunt us, but motivates as well!

Judgment is both individual and universal. "We will *all* stand before the judgment seat of God." (Romans 14:10)

---

[31] Cited in *Globequake,* by Wallace Henley, 51.
[32] Dinesh D'Souza, *Life After Death,* 166-167.

Judgment is also part of your first step in Heaven. "Each person dies only once and after that comes judgment," says Hebrews 9:27. (NLT)

1. *Ontological Judgment*

"Ontology" is the study of being. Therefore the first judgment question at the Throne of God is: *Does this individual have being, existence, and citizenship in the Kingdom of Heaven?*

As we have seen in other chapters, our being arises from God's Zoe-Life within our spirit. (Genesis 2:7) Our existence in a given realm is a result of our being "there." When we actualize our sin nature by willfully sinning, however, we expel God's Zoe-Life from our human spirit, which was made to be the "Holy of Holies" of our body, the Temple of God. All that is left is psychic-physical existence. We still have a soul, and the functions of mind, emotion, and will, housed in our body, but without the Zoe of God through the Holy Spirit, we do not have the fullness of being, but mere existence in material form within the spacetime universe.

The horror is that we do not have being or existence in the Kingdom of Heaven. We are at that point "*dead* in… trespasses and sins." (Ephesians 2:1, emphasis added)

The Lamb's Book of Life, seen in the Revelation visions, is the "birth record" of Heaven. It is the ontological chronicle of all those who have being and existence there. Only "those whose names are written in the Lamb's Book of Life" are permitted to enter and live in Heaven. (Revelation 21:27) All others are assigned to the "Outside" where reside "the unclean" and practitioners of "abomination and lying," those who intentionally and willfully pursue a continual lifestyle of "sexual immorality, impure thoughts, eagerness for lustful pleasure, idolatry, participation in demonic activities, hostility, quarreling, jealousy, outbursts of anger, selfish ambition, divisions, the feeling that everyone is wrong except those in (one's) own little group, envy, drunkenness, wild parties, and other kinds of sin." (Galatians 5:19-21 NLT)

How does one get entered into the Lamb's Book of Life? The answer: since it is a record of births, you must be born. You cannot exist in a realm where you have no being. Therefore you must have a "new birth", you must be "born again" with a Heaven-style birth. This, of course, was Jesus' whole point to Nicodemus in John 3.

The new birth is that of "re-generation." It is being born again into "newness (new quality) of life." The Greek term is the lovely word we encountered earlier, *paliggenesia*, from *palig* ("again") and *genesis* ("beginning" or "birth"). Christ "saved us... by the washing of regeneration and renewing of the Holy Spirit," says Titus 3:5. This results in being born into "newness of life." (Romans 6:4) "Newness" is from the Greek word that means "new in quality," not merely new in time, or merely novel.

When we receive Christ we not only climb up on the cross with Him and receive the atonement of justification, but we also crawl into the manger with Him, and are born in Christ with His quality of Zoe-Life. We rise again with Him at His resurrection into this new quality of life. We lost our innocence in the Garden, but we get it back on the cross. We lost our Zoe in the Garden, but we get it back in the manger and the empty tomb!

2. Functional Judgment

Those in Christ do not come before the Great White Throne of ontological judgment, but they do undergo functional judgment. Paul gives detail in 1 Corinthians 3:11-15,

> ... no one can lay any other foundation than the one we already have — Jesus Christ. Now anyone who builds on that foundation may use gold, silver, jewels, wood, hay, or straw. But there is going to come a time of testing at the judgment day to see what kind of work each builder has done. Everyone's work will be put through the fire to see whether or not it keeps its value. If the work survives the fire, that builder will receive a reward. But if the work is burned up, the builder will suffer great loss. The builders themselves will be saved, but like someone escaping through a wall of flames. (NLT)

Functional judgment therefore is the evaluation of our function through the spiritual gifts and other resources God entrusted to us while we were living on earth. All humans, as God's image-bearers, are put in the created world for purpose. The purpose is linked to God's Kingdom and its advance in the world. Tragically, the fall into sin separates us from our original purpose and destiny. However, when we receive Christ, our purpose and destiny are restored to our lives, along with all necessary to accomplish the mission for which God placed us in the world. This is why we are allotted spiritual gifts according to our assignment, material resources, and opportunity. The judgment of our works therefore is on the basis of what we did with God's treasures entrusted to us to advance His Kingdom of righteousness, peace, and joy (Romans 14:17), and bring people to Christ and citizenship in His Kingdom.

Though Harvey Weinstein is not a follower of Christ, an episode from his life can help us understand what the functional judgment may feel like. Weinstein is a top Hollywood movie producer. He is in total conformity with the movie-world's leftism. He despises the Second Amendment right to bear arms, and loathes the National Rifle Association. Weinstein revealed on a nationally syndicated radio program that he was going to produce a film that would make the NRA wish it were not alive.[33] But then Weinstein faced a shocker: he had produced films full of violence—and guns. Weinstein told his interviewer he was backing away from violence in his movies. The movie mogul realized that his works didn't line up with his beliefs.

The standard of judgment for our works will be eternity itself. Only those we achieved that endure in Heaven and eternity make it through the flames. People who

---

[33] http://www.foxnews.com/entertainment/2014/01/16/harvey-weinstein-has-secret-film-project-to-destroy-nra/

trusted Christ for their salvation but had almost no eternal Kingdom works on earth get to remain in Heaven on the basis of Christ's justification, but they have a lesser degree of reward. Yet such people are not jealous because they live in an atmosphere of perfect love. Because they love all in the heavenly "community of saints" as intimate family, their joy for those who receive great reward is as exhilarating (and even more) as when, back on earth, they exulted in the successes of their own spouses, children, or other special loved ones that may have exceeded their own. Parents entered into the exhilaration of a kid who made a three-point long shot in a basketball game, or received a college scholarship, or a spouse whose job performance was crowned with rewards and recognition, or a cherished friend who won a marathon. In Heaven, we all love one another at that level, and celebrate the accomplishments and rewards of others, not because it is as if they were our own, but precisely because they were not. True love focuses on the other, not on self-acclaim or achievement.

How the judging is done

When John first sees Christ in the Revelation vision, he is struck by those eyes that are like "flaming fire". Though the Bible is composed of 66 books it is unitary, a whole. Therefore, Zechariah 4 gives us more detail about God's eyes. In a vision, the Prophet sees a stand bearing seven lamps. He asks the angel who has brought the vision the meaning of its elements.

The lamps symbolize the penetrating eyes of God: "these are the eyes of the Lord which range to and fro throughout the earth." (Zechariah 4:10) Further, God's eyes see perfectly and completely. "Seven" is the number of perfection. God's searching eyes miss nothing. In the beginning, God's eyes look at His creation with satisfaction and pleasure. (Genesis 1:31) Think of an artist standing back to look at his completed work and feeling the satisfaction of a masterful accomplishment. Then, throughout history, God's eyes search out the people open to Him, those He can strengthen. (2 Chronicles 16:9)

But the revelation through Zechariah shows that God's eyes are also the means of judgment. The key is in verse 10: "... these seven will be glad when they see the *plumb line* in the hand of Zerubbabel — these are the eyes of the LORD which range to and fro throughout the earth." (Emphasis added)

We humans lack the perfection and completeness of vision with which God's eyes function. I learned this many years ago in building a cypress fence around the backyard of our home then near Mobile, Alabama. I labored for days to build the frame around the perimeter. Finally I began to attach the slats. I carefully "plumbed" each of the first dozen or so vertical boards. Then it occurred to me that the fence perimeter was large, and that if I measured the vertical alignment of each one it would take me forever to finish the fence. Not even cypress-wood would last that long, I figured. So, I "eyeballed" each slat I attached for straightness, and the project swept forward. At about fence-slat 27 I saw something was wrong. The board was not straightly aligned. I stepped back, and could see the problem: Because I had not plumbed the boards, but merely depended on my eyesight, I failed to see the nuanced tilt that had gradually entered the project until it finally increased to the point of being visible to my limited vision.

So the linkage of the "plumb-line" to the vision of the seven eyes of God shows us that when the Lord judges He misses no nuance, no small "tilt" toward sin and away from Him. His judgment is sweeping and all-inclusive. No wonder Hebrews 10:31 says, "It is a terrifying thing to fall into the hands of the living God"! But there is no terror for the person in Christ.

The first four-by-four post I sunk into the ground for the fence-frame was perfectly vertical. It was in complete conformity to the laws of geometry. I had used a literal plumb-line to position the post. Then, as I worked it into the ground and poured concrete around it I constantly checked vertical alignment. I did this with each post. The first slat I attached to the completed frame was also perfectly upright by the principles of geometry. It completely fulfilled the "law". Suppose I, as the judge, looked back at all the slats out of alignment, and had the power to transfer the uprightness of the first perfectly upright board to all the others? My judging eyes would suddenly see them all as perfectly vertical and as totally aligned with the laws of geometry as the first, carefully measured slat.

This is why the person in Christ does not have to be terrified in the presence of the living God, nor fear the judgment to come. When you take your first step in Heaven and are instantly probed by the completeness of God's vision, if you are in Christ, He sees you as upright as the perfect Son of God!

Our lives on earth are not only for the purpose of advancing God's Kingdom in the world but also preparatory for Heaven. The decisions we make now about living directly impact our dying. "It is the seeking heart that determines our eternal destiny. In the heart heaven or hell are decided," writes Peter Kreeft.[34]

As the Apostle Peter contemplates the new heavens and new earth "in which righteousness dwells" purely and totally, he suddenly cries, "what holy, godly lives you should be living!" (2 Peter 3:11 NLT) Gordon Fee writes about the "now, but not yet" reality of life in Christ. The Holy Spirit, he says, "reconstitutes God's people anew and empowers us to live the life of the future in our between-the-times existence—between the time of Christ's first and second coming."[35]

Think of an astronaut guiding a spacecraft back from a moon mission. Earth is far ahead, a blue jewel against the backdrop of space. Landing on earth is still days away in the astronaut's future, but all the decisions he or she makes in their present moment is guided by and in the context of that future arrival. The slightest misdirection of the spaceship could result in missing the narrow window in spacetime that

---

[34] Peter Kreeft, *Heaven, the Heart's Deepest Longing*.
[35] Gordon Fee, *Paul, the Spirit, and the People of God*.

gets the vessel and its crew in an orbit that will enable them to land on earth. So the way we "steer and step" in the *now* determines the outcome of our *not yet*.

Today, the present moment, is the day of salvation (both present and future). (2 Corinthians 6:2) The bottom line is that your first step in Heaven begins now. Every step is a footfall, but every footfall results from lifting the leg and putting it forward. *Now* is the time to set your foot so that its first step is in Heaven.

Chapter 7

WHOM WILL YOU KNOW?

On your first step in Heaven you will not only see your loved ones who died in the Lord, but know them at a level you could never have perceived on earth.

Seeing is wonderful. I can be among dozens of people I love greatly, but when my eyes spot Irene in the crowd, immediately I feel a lift, a joy that I cannot express.

Something remarkable happened the first time I saw her in 1959, when she was 16 and I was 17. It was the first day of a citywide church camp where I was working. I was standing in a hut with other young men on the staff. Truthfully, we were scanning the new female arrivals. Irene was at least 125 yards away, walking with some of her friends on the campus. I saw only her, and I knew that somehow she was special.

We courted that week, but the decisive moment came one evening when we sat on the steps of an old wooden building under an Alabama moon. Other teens were scampering all around us, but it was as if we were the only two people on the planet. We talked a long time, and really began to know each other in spirit and soul. A bond was formed that night in 1959 that was formalized in 1961, when we married.

Seeing is wonderful, but knowing is far better. How often has a parent sat with a troubled child or elderly confused parent wishing they could really know what was going on inside? How many times has a teacher struggling with a hyperactive student desired to get into the child's brain to see what is blocking the ability to pay attention? How frequently has a pastor or other counselor yearned to know the root of the churning and fear in the core of a needy person?

In Heaven we will see at a level we cannot comprehend in this world. We will know people not just on the surface, but at their core. That may be intimidating to most of us. Do we really want the person wearing the silly hat to know what we really meant when we called it "truly remarkable"? Do we want everyone knowing what's burrowed into our heart—the resentments, lusts, lies, and doubts? "The heart is more deceitful than all else and is desperately sick," writes Jeremiah. (Jeremiah 17:9)

In Heaven, however, we have a new heart. It is as pure as Christ's. Nothing is in that heart that would bring us shame. In Heaven we live in exhilarating honesty. We will never again say, "No one understands me." Everyone will read us like a book, and the story will be wonderful. We will be appreciated, and will know and regard others in the same way.

We are not resting this study primarily on Near Death Experiences (NDE) because that is not a sufficiently authoritative base on which to stand. Such experiences can be a side effect of drugs and medications, a dream, or some other subjective phenomenon. Rather, we are looking entirely to Scripture. However, there are many NDEs that align with God's Word, and these are trustworthy.

Take, for example, the case of Dr. Michael Minotti, a North Carolina surgeon. After a period of skepticism he concluded that NDEs were real because of what he had experienced with people who had died and come back. "There is far more evidence that they are real than they are not," he said. Among the reasons is the NDEs are "life changing," and "not like having a mere dream."

Dr. Minotti tells of experiences with

> "blind people who have had a near death experience; they've been clinically dead, and have been resuscitated and left their bodies and saw for the first time. They've explained in detail the resuscitation efforts, which they in no way could have known."[36]

St. Augustine, after much study, came to this conclusion:

> "We have not lost our dear ones who have departed from this life, but have merely sent them ahead of us, so we shall depart and come to that life where they will be more than ever

---

[36] http://m.christianpost.com/news/woman-claims-she-saw-heaven-while-clinically-dead-divine-encounters-are-real-says-doctor-113969/

dear as they will be *better known to us*, and where we shall love them without any fear of parting." (Emphasis added)

The Bible shows that everyone sees in Heaven, including those who have been blind on earth, like those Dr. Minotti worked with. But where does Augustine get the idea that not only will we see them but that "they will be better known to us"? Perhaps it is from perhaps the most important passage regarding the visual feast of Heaven, 1 John 3:2-3:

> Beloved, now we are children of God, and it has not appeared as yet what we will be. We know that when He appears, we will be like Him, because we will see Him just as He is. And everyone who has this hope *fixed* on Him purifies himself, just as He is pure.

This passage highlights the difference between seeing and knowing. In Heaven we not only see others *externally*, but we behold their very *essence*. The Revelation visions show that Jesus' external appearance is beyond glory and beauty, unimaginable. A human here on earth cannot look upon such radiant magnificence. Our hearts would beat so fast they would explode. But in Heaven we will see Jesus something as the disciples on the Mount of Transfiguration could see Him—except better. There must have been some shielding to keep Peter, James, and John from dying for the same reason Moses had to be hidden in the cleft of the rock when the glory of God passed by.

But in Heaven we will not need to be shielded. We will see Him as He is. And if we see Him as He is there is every evidence that we see and really know others in the magnitude of their purity and holiness, because all their sin will have been removed. And they will see you the same way.

The little boy in the blockbuster book, *Heaven Is For Real*, saw people while he was apparently dead and in Heaven who had died before he was born. He not only saw them, but knew them to such a degree his parents were amazed when he told them. Again, this is one of those NDEs we can trust because of the alignment of the experience with biblical revelation.

My mother was born in January, 1915. Her father had died just months before, in 1914. My mother's mother passed away in 1941, one month before I was born. I have so often wondered about them. In Heaven I will know them instantly. It will be as if we had always been together.

Wishful thinking, or reality?

But is this mere wishful thinking? We must always come back to the crucial question: Is there biblical authority for believing that we will see and know our loved ones when we step into Heaven? Let's take a look in the Scriptures.

Let's begin where the Bible does, in the Book of Genesis. Prior to the fall into sin, Eden was an extension into the material world of the Kingdom of Heaven. The lovely picture of God walking with His image-bearers "in the cool of the day" (Genesis 3:8) shows the capacity for movement and fellowship between the trans-natural and natural dimensions of Heaven and earth. Evil—the choice of the humans, not God—carved out a huge chasm between Heaven and earth.

The Bible, however, reveals there is coming in the natural world's kronos-time a complete restoration of earth and the universe to their original mint condition—a "New Heaven" and a "New Earth." This means that all the pre-fall conditions of Paradise will be universal. Heaven's kairos-time will overlap nature's kronos-time, and there will be no more sequential movement toward death and decay.

Further, the same level of intimacy that existed in pre-fall Eden will prevail in the New Earth. Adam and Eve saw each other and knew each other. Before sin, when Adam's eyes were clear, seeing things as God sees them, the Lord brought newly created Eve to Adam, who shouts,

> "This is now bone of my bones,
> And flesh of my flesh;
> She shall be called Woman,
> Because she was taken out of Man."
> (Genesis 2:23)

Acts 3 gives us a key insight into Heaven. The period between the first and second coming of Christ will be the season of repentance and grace. God will give humanity opportunity to turn from the sin that separates men and women from Him, and receive the grace won at immense cost by Jesus on the cross. Therefore, Christ will not return until the "period of restoration of all things about which God spoke by the mouth of His holy prophets from ancient time." (Acts 3:21)

"Restoration" is the sublimely beautiful Greek, *palig genesia*. Basically, the term means to "begin again." The Bible is telling us that there will be another creative moment for the universe and our world.

Scientists speculate that at the beginning of our present universe all the matter was as an infinitely small melted mass. The compression was so intense, atomic reactions occurred, resulting in a "Big Bang". The Bible gives us more detail: That vast explosive moment was ignited by God's creative Logos, His Word spoken into the void.

So, writes Simon Peter, this present world will once more melt away as kairos overtakes kronos, and the spatial nature of Heaven overwhelms the spacetime universe. The result will be the new creation, where all will be as they were in the beginning when sin had not corrupted humanity and nature.

This is the Heaven that already awaits in kairos-time. And Jesus, the Christ, the Logos, returns, "God will bring with Him those who have fallen asleep in Jesus." (1 Thessalonians 4:14)

From the kronos perspective it would seem that the lives of our deceased loved ones have ended. But that is only because of our limited view. God knows that it is merely like sleep with respect to earth-time. "Each night when I go to sleep, I die," said Gandhi. "And the next morning when I wake up I am reborn." Our family and friends who have died in the Lord might seem "dead to the world" from our perspective, but in Heaven they are vibrantly alive and aware. And when kairos becomes the time-quality of earth, they are with those who haven't yet crossed over because those who've gone on before us are already in Heaven-time.

And because this is the *palig genesia*, the New Earth that has the nature of the Old Earth before the fall, we will know our loved ones as much as Adam and Eve knew one another and together as well as individually knew God. The primary difference is that we are neither married nor given in marriage in Heaven because we are in a state of fellowship and intimacy that is far greater than the marriage relationship (if possible)!

A few weeks ago from the time I am writing, Irene and I had an experience that made us profoundly aware of the beauty of God's ways. Back in July, we had to fly to Birmingham to do the memorial service for our best friend there. Frank and Nona Parsons had been co-laborers in the church we served, overseas traveling companions, and even business partners. Frank had been a candidate for Mayor of Birmingham, and I had led his campaign, with Irene and Nona working as hard as we did. I was shattered when Frank died because he was like a blood brother.

Then a mere six months later Irene and I were once again jetting to Birmingham to do the memorial service for Nona. The day after the service, before we flew back to Houston, Frank and Nona's grown son asked us to come to their house because there was memorabilia he thought we would want. As we sorted through the items, I was struck by the story we are all writing as we live in this world, and its finality.

Then it hit me: The way God sees it from where I was standing in their big garage was as if Frank and Nona had just gone upstairs to take a nap, yet from God's perspective in Heaven He sees them fully alive and awake, enjoying His presence and one another's company. Further, God already sees and Frank and Nona are already experiencing the presence of us all, because in kairos, all that is to *be* already *is*!

This has to be at least part of what Paul meant when the Holy Spirit inspired him to write,

> "No eye has seen, no ear has heard,
> and no mind has imagined
> what God has prepared
> for those who love him..."
> (1 Corinthians 2:9 NLT)

In some ways, the post-resurrection appearances of Jesus were previews of the way we know one another in Heaven. In his incarnation, Jesus Christ put aside the prerogatives of His Deity. (Philippians 2) He was and is the

Eternal Logos (Word) of God, the Son forever, and yet He entered kronos. The two dimensions of Heaven and Earth were linked in Jesus of Nazareth. He inhabited the two levels of time simultaneously, but in His incarnation, He *functioned* primarily in kronos, earth-time, with all its restrictions. But in His essence, He never lost His Heavenly *Being*.

That changed in His resurrection. He moved about in kronos, but was already living in kairos. We saw earlier John's words in 1 John 3 that "when He appears, we will be like Him, because we will see Him just as He is." Therefore, if Jesus' disciples usually recognized Him even though He was in His resurrected heavenly body, and if "we will be like Him" when we are in the resurrection body into which we step when we first enter Heaven, then our loved ones will see and know us and us them.

Jonathan Edwards, the great 18th century spiritual leader and Great Awakening evangelist in America's earliest days, thought about this a great deal. He wanted earnestly to believe—as we all do—that we know our loved ones in Heaven. He did what we are seeking to do in this study, and searched the Scriptures and meditated on them. After many years of contemplation, here is what Jonathan Edwards wrote:

> "As the streams tend to the ocean, so all these are tending to the great ocean of infinite purity and bliss. The progress of time does but bear them on to its blessedness; and us, if we are

holy, to be united to them there. Every gem which death rudely tears away from us here is a glorious jewel forever shining there; every Christian friend that goes before us from this world, is a ransomed spirit waiting to welcome us in heaven. There will be the infant of days that we have lost below, through grace to be found above; there the Christian father, and mother, and wife, and child, and friend, with whom we shall renew the holy fellowship of the saints, which was interrupted by death here, but shall be commenced again in the upper sanctuary, and then shall never end."

Chapter 8

WHAT ABOUT THOSE YOU WON'T SEE?

"You can't go home again." That's the title of a classic 20th century book written by Tom Wolfe.

As many of us have found, we can go back to the physical location, but not back home again to moments and relationships once dear to us. Soulless time crawls across the landscape of space like armies of locusts devouring everything in their path.

If you live long enough there is a sad sequence you pass through. You move away from home in your younger days. A few months or a year later you go back, and your stay is full of visits to friends and family. Irene used to laugh when we journeyed home to Birmingham, because she knew I would be driving all over the city seeing old relatives, friends, and former work associates.

But on a later trip you enter another segment of the sequence. The many shrinks to the lesser. Next time the lesser is fewer, and then to not-so-many. Then there comes a bittersweet time when the not-so-many shrinks into the almost none. Where once two weeks was not enough to see everyone, go out to dinner, spend the night, gather with all the friends and family for parties, there comes a time when two days back home are all that are needed. And then for some, there's no point in going back home at all. The old home place is gone. No one is left back there for you to visit.

In the last chapter we talked about whom we would know on our first step in Heaven. Tom Wolfe, though not a Christian writer, caught the joy of those reunions when he put these beautiful words in the mouth of a character in *You Can't Go Home Again:*

> "Something has spoken to me in the night... and told me that I shall die... Saying "(Death is) to lose the earth you know for greater knowing; to lose the life you have, for greater life; to leave the friends you loved, for greater loving; to find a land more kind than home, more large than earth.

It's wonderful to think of all those people we will see and know again—but in an even better, more expansive way, as we saw in the previous chapter. Now, however, we have to come to a hard question that gnaws at our hearts: *What about those we don't see on our first step in Heaven... or upon any of the steps after that?* Will we call out their names in frantic hope they will answer? Will we search every particle of Heaven's territory looking for them?

What if our search turns up empty? What if we have to accept the darkest fact that they simply are not there? Bereaved people know it takes a long time to even begin to be healed of grief, and often the healing is not total. Will the absence from Heaven of those we love provoke another, even worse grief? Will we spend eternity mourning over those not there?

Perhaps all of us would have to admit that there are people we love so much that if they are not in Heaven we are not sure we even want to be there. So if they are not present, how can Heaven be Heaven for us? If they are not in Heaven, but separated from us by an uncrossable dimension, what's the significance of there being "no sea" of uttermost separation in Heaven? After all, crossing a wide sea is possible, but trans-dimensional travel is impossible. "Between us and you there is a great chasm fixed, so that those who wish to come over from here to you will not be able, and that none may cross over from there to us," says Abraham to the rich man in Hades in Jesus' parable. (Luke 16:26-27)

What about those we don't see when we arrive in Heaven and will never see because they are not there? What about *us* in the midst of this reality? Will we be broken-hearted forever?

We know the answer to that. Revelation 21 says there is no grieving in Heaven. There is no mournful weeping, and God wipes all the tears from our eyes. (Revelation 7:17; 21:4) I've read and heard many accounts of Near Death Experiences (NDEs), but I have not known one report in which a person returned grieving over those loved ones who died before them that they did *not* see in Heaven.

The Bible gives us clear information about this.

1. *Those who are not there do not exist there, and have never existed there, and you do not grieve for what has never existed.*

One of the saddest situations in the contemporary world is the fact that millions of births are never registered—as many as 51 million babies in a recent year, two-fifths of all those born worldwide in that period. In effect, those people don't "exist" when it comes to accessing rights and privileges of citizenship. They are people without a country, unable in many places to get an education, marry, vote, qualify for a passport, and enjoy many other prerogatives belonging to a citizen.

With so many children deprived of these rights because of their births not being registered, the United Nations got involved in establishing the Convention on the Rights of the Child. "The child shall be registered immediately after birth and shall have the right from birth to a *name* (and) the right to acquire a *nationality*," among others. (Emphasis added)

Revelation 2:17 speaks of us having a "new name" in Heaven, given by God Himself. That's our "birth name", not the name we carry in our earthly life. It is the "new name" that is recorded in Heaven's book. So Heaven's Book of Life officially lists those who "exist" there and have all the rights of heavenly citizenship.

Earth is the "delivery room" where the "new birth" occurs. It is while we live in this world that we make our decision for or against Christ. The moment we receive His Life, we are re-generated, "born again" in and through Him, and our new birth names are written in Heaven's book of life. So, in Philippians 4:3, Paul refers to his "(contemporary) fellow workers whose names are (already) written in the book of life."

Every time I vote I go to my precinct where there is a roster with my name already printed. Yet when I decide to cast my ballot, and arrive at the registration table, I have to place my signature next to my pre-printed name. If I don't do that I am not given the ticket that allows me into the voting booth, even though my name was already printed in the voting roster for my precinct.

So our decision to receive Christ is our intentional participation in God's foreknowledge. Making that decision means we are affirming our choice, just as when I register my name on the voters' list I am declaring my citizenship and signaling my choice to cast a ballot. Those who make that decision for Christ will never have their names erased from the book of life! (Revelation 3:5)

However, those whose names are not written in the book of life simply are not there, as we noted in a previous chapter. Revelation 21:27 puts it bluntly that "only those whose names are written in the Lamb's book of life" inhabit Heaven.

Thus there is no possibility of us remembering those who do not and did not exist in the world we inhabit, which at that point will be Heaven.

2. *The former world has passed away and the memory of it.*

God says in Isaiah 65:17 that He will create new heavens and new earth, "and the former things will not be remembered or come to mind."

Arthur Clarke, the science fiction writer, spins the story of a 10-year old boy who is part of a colony that escaped an earth dying from nuclear war, a world that had become nothing more than a radioactive dump. One day his father takes him up onto a mountain on the planet where they are living. Out in space he sees earth, a point of light far away. It seems so beautiful until he recognizes the radiance is from the very nuclear destruction that killed all the inhabitants except those of the colony.

And yet because of the wonderful stories his father had told him, the child longed to go to earth. Then came time for the boy and his dad to leave the high peak where earth could be seen so well. "He did not look back as they began their homeward journey," writes Clarke. "He could not bear to see the cold glory of the crescent Earth fade from the rocks around him."

But that's not the way it is in Heaven. We won't look back wistfully at earth, and all the people and memories we had there. That's because the earth doesn't exist and in the mind and emotions of your new soul, never existed. 2 Peter 3:10 says the day will come when the earth will "pass away". *Parerchomai* is the New Testament Greek word. As we saw in an earlier chapter, it refers to something—a person, object, state of existence—fading from view until even its memory is gone.

In 1946, just after World War 2, my daddy took me down to Mobile Bay to show me the naval vessels home from the war sheltering there. I remember because I had a water pistol, and was so thrilled to go down to the edge of the Bay, fill up my squirt gun, and fire away at the battleships and cruisers.

I am sure I saw freighters too, shrinking away on the horizon. And when they were gone their very memory was blotted from my childish mind. This is the idea embedded in *parerchomai*. From the perspective of Heaven's shores our life on earth and all our experiences pass into non-existence with the disappearing vessel on which we once sailed turbulently through kronos-time on the ocean of space.

3. *The past vanishes in the light of the glory of the continual present of Heaven.*

Revelation 7 speaks of those before God's Throne in Heaven and says they won't hunger or thirst, or feel the heat sapping away their vitality. The key phrase is in verse 17, which refers to "the Lamb at the center of the Throne." That will be the whole field of our focus in Heaven. There simply will be no room in our new souls for memories and feelings from the life on earth. Everything is overwhelmed in the magnitude of His manifest presence.

Light a match in the depths of Carlsbad Caverns and it looks like the sun. Hold the burning match against the brilliance of the rising sun, and the pathetic flicker is engulfed in the roaring radiance. The brilliance of the Lamb at the center of the Throne overpowers all other lights, including those that illuminate our memories of life back on earth.

There are great truths we can distill from these facts.

As I write these words one of my granddaughters has just discovered she is pregnant, and that Irene and I will be great-grandparents. When she told us we shouted for joy. There is a baby in her womb! We all anticipate the day we can cradle the child in our arms. Though the conceived child is little more than a month old as I write, it exists in our world though we cannot see it yet. But we have other grandchildren who have not yet conceived children. Those not conceived physically in the body are not conceived yet in our minds either. Thus we don't miss them because they are not "here" in any form. You will not grieve in Heaven over those not there because, again, you are in a dimension where family and friends who were not "born again" while on earth never existed.

The "circle" of family and friends that we will be part of in Heaven exists right now in the earth. These are the relationships you will experience in Heaven. They are the people you will see and know. Those among even your family who are not in that circle of heavenly citizenship and who choose never to be are not in that circle in Heaven. You will not miss what you did not know and experience.

Jesus' parable about Lazarus and the rich man in Hades that we discussed above also sheds much light at this point. It also reminds me of another grandchild story.

When our youngest granddaughter was born Irene and I had the joy of babysitting her, as we had our five other grandkids. Sometimes she would stay the night with us so her parents could take a trip. If she cried in the wee hours I would wake up, and lift her gently from her crib. Then I would sit down in a big brown rocker-recliner in our den, and hold her to my chest as I rocked and sang to her.

We still have the big brown rocker-recliner, though the child, as I write these words, is 17. But when I think of that special time in her infancy I understand why "Abraham's bosom" (or lap) came to signify Heaven. Abraham was the father of both Jews and Arabs. But especially is he the patriarch of people who walk in the Covenant initially pointing to Jesus Christ and ultimately fulfilled in Him.

In Jesus' striking parable, Lazarus, a poor man back on earth, is now resting in Abraham's lap while a rich man who had rejected God was in Hades—in Christian understanding synonymous with Hell. We learn important things here:

1. *Travel between Heaven and Hell is impossible.* The "great chasm" is not merely a canyon, but an impassable, unreachable distance. Further, there is a categorical barrier to this passage: one who has the life-nature of Hell cannot exist in the life-nature of Heaven any more than an ice-cube could survive in a blast furnace.
2. *While Lazarus has no awareness of the rich man, the rich man can see Lazarus and the blessing he is enjoying in Heaven.* It may be that among the greatest torments of Hell is that its inhabitants can see

into Heaven and have constant awareness of what they have missed. There is no indication in anything Jesus says, however, that Lazarus could see the rich man in Hell or anyone else there, including family and friends of Lazarus who might not have made the choice of Heaven while on earth.

3. *While Lazarus does not remember and therefore does not grieve those of his family and friends who may not have chosen God's Way to Heaven, the rich man is very much aware of his family members still on earth.* The passionate hope of the rich man is that someone will warn his loved ones to make choices that would insure they would not come to Hell—as much as he doubtless yearns to see them.

Many years ago our family was on a ski trip. Some of us were skilled on the slopes, others not. One of the most harrowing moments of my life occurred as I was riding back up the mountain on a ski lift. Suddenly I saw my daughter down below fall and slide rapidly toward a collision with the skier ahead. To my horror I saw the person about to be knocked down was my wife. I was about 50 feet above them on the lift. The sense of helplessness was distressing. They couldn't even hear my voice. There was no way I could rescue them. By God's grace the collision wasn't as bad as it appeared it would be. However, I never again want the experience of seeing a loved one on a collision course with tragedy and not be able to help.

The rich man in Hell feels an urgency he should have allowed himself to experience in his life on earth. Now he wants "father Abraham" to get the message of the urgency of salvation to his family still alive on earth. This is an urgency you and I need to feel now. Billy Graham points to this need when he writes: "The terrible possibility that our loved ones might miss heaven should motivate us to earnestly pray and lovingly witness to them while there is still time in this life for them to experience salvation."

But there are other hard questions: What about our family and friends who had no capacity to hear and respond to Christ's invitation of salvation—babies, mentally handicapped, and others with limitations of comprehension? Will they be in Heaven? Will we see and know them when we step into Heaven?

These are questions we probe in the next chapter.

Chapter 9

WILL WE SEE LOVED ONES WHO NEVER HEARD THE GOSPEL?

The young mother and father grieved the loss of their still-born baby as if they had known her for years. Though they had two healthy children, their third had died in the womb. Nevertheless, they gave the little girl a name taken straight from the Bible, and asked me to be with them at a graveside service.

I always tell people we are not conducting a "funeral" but celebrating a life. To prepare for a service I always go to those who knew the person best—first, his or her Creator, and second family members. We talk about all the individual's accomplishments, and past experiences loved ones had with the loved one. Then, at the service, I link elements of the person's journey in this world with the scriptural insights stirred in me by the Holy Spirit.

But how do you do that with a child whose whole life was spent in his or her mother's womb, or who may have lived just moments after birth? If it is necessary to be "born again" to have one's name written in Heaven's book of life, how can I assure grieving parents they will see their child there, though he or she couldn't make the crucial decision to receive Christ?

As a high school student I went on Sunday afternoon visits with my church youth group to a home caring for severely impaired people. In the 1950s such facilities were not as sophisticated as now. On my first visits I was shocked at the appearance and limitations of some of the patients. Several seemed only to have involuntary brain activity, while others demonstrated varying degrees of limited awareness.

What was the point in giving them the Gospel? The question gnawed at me at times.

I preached my first sermons at the Jimmy Hale Mission in downtown Birmingham, Alabama. Most of the attendees were there because being present at the chapel service was a prerequisite to getting a meal and bed. Many were drunk or drugged into oblivion, and could barely sit up. How could they "come and reason together" about sin and Christ's salvation?

And yet every time I preached at the mission, a man I will call Mr. O'Malley was always there, singing hymns in a high falsetto. He had mental and emotional limitations, but prayed earnestly for the drunks around him. Perhaps it was because Mr. O'Malley remembered that he had been able to hear and respond to the Gospel years before when he was in a stupor.

But the most complex questions of all arise from the soul-crunching suicide of a beloved family member or friend. In almost four decades as a pastor, I have dealt with this at least a half dozen times. I look into the faces of grieving parents, or spouses, or children, and read the often unspoken questions: What went wrong? More important, *is there any hope I will see him/her in Heaven?*

How, as a pastor, can I give assurance of their child's salvation to parents grieving a little one who died too young to make the decision to be "born again"? How can I assure family members about the eternal security of a loved one bound to a bed or wheelchair who seems to grasp nothing? How can I give assurance to people whose dearest ones have destroyed their minds with drugs and intoxicants, or taken their own lives in acts of suicide?

And yet I do give that assurance often, even in some cases of suicide. *You will see family and friends in Heaven who, because of some incapacitation, couldn't respond to the Gospel while alive on Earth.*

Let me tell you why.

1. **First, a hard fact: sin is objective reality not subjective opinion.**

A physician tells a woman she has inoperable cancer. However, she is in an early stage of the disease and feels no effects. She decides the diagnosis is merely the doctor's subjective opinion. She refuses to deal with the cancer, and months later it kills her.

Many people treat sin this way—especially in a culture endlessly preaching that morality is relative. "What is bad for you may not be bad for me," is the mantra repeated nowadays through media, in the classroom, on dates, and even in some churches.

The word "is" is humanity's big moral problem, thinks Robert Anton Wilson, author of the book, *Nature's God*. "I don't know what anything 'is', I only know how it seems to me at this moment," he says. This is highly descriptive of the naïve subjectivism that drives our postmodern culture. The problem is that sin is an "is" in the same way the Law of Gravity is an "is".[37] James 1:15 gets to the core of it when it reveals that "when lust has conceived, it gives birth to sin; and when sin is accomplished, it brings forth death." Death is cold, hard fact.

John Owen, the 17th century Puritan leader, understood the severe objectivity of sin when he wrote,

> "Sin aims always at the utmost; every time it rises up to tempt or entice, if it has its own way it will go out to the utmost sin in that kind. Every unclean thought or glance would be adultery if it could, every thought of unbelief would be atheism if allowed to develop. Every rise of lust, if it has its way reaches the height of villainy; it is like the grave that is never satisfied. The deceitfulness of sin is seen in that it is modest in its first proposals but when it prevails it hardens men's hearts, and brings them to ruin."[38]

---

[37] Robert Anton Wilson, *Nature's God,* New Falcon Publications, 2007.
[38] John Owen, *The Mortification of Sin,* Trinity Press, 2013.

No one would dismiss the seriousness of a cancer and its effects simply because the affected person didn't have the capacity to know about cancer and its potential cures. Sin has to be dealt with, even in those who cannot understand.

So how can we give assurance of Heaven regarding those with no capacity to understand the Gospel, and respond to it through repentance and trusting Christ for salvation?

Keep reading!

2. *Sin is not "imputed" where there is no law.* (Romans 5:13)

The question is: At what point is sin "imputed" (charged to one's account)? Paul is not suggesting that in the absence of law sin loses its objective character. However, the Holy Spirit is revealing that there is a point at which a man or woman actually recognizes sin in light of the law, tries to turn off or throw a rock at the glaring spotlight, and chooses sin.

The sin-nature every human possesses because of our heritage from Adam guarantees we will at some point make the sin-choice, just as having a propensity to catch a cold makes it inevitable that if we choose to go out with wet hair on a cold day we will come down with a cold.

When one acts upon the sin-nature and intentionally, willfully makes the sin-choice, the person actually *becomes* a sinner. Further, because the sin is willful, the individual is no longer held up by the big parachute of grace (more in a moment) but becomes like a person leaping from an airplane wearing an iron suit. To put it another way: *When we make the choice called for by the sin-nature we swap the wings of glory for the iron suit of objective legal guilt.*

Some (limited) illustrations

Speaking of parachutes: think of a skydiver on his first solo leap. Due to a rush of oxygen and hefty wind that socks him, Jack is momentarily giddy and disoriented. He decides he can fly on his own, jettisons the parachute before opening it and flaps his arms. Had he opened the chute, the law of gravity might have not judged him quite as severely, but in abandoning himself to the sky Jack has broken the natural law, and turned his destiny over to its cold indifference.

Or consider Bill and Jane, who are going on a big overseas trip. International flight tickets are expensive, and so they study itineraries and fares carefully. Finally, with nerves on edge, Bill pulls out his credit card and sits down at his computer to make reservations online. His anxiety rises as he knows he must get the itinerary right. Once he clicks the "reserve" button for that less expensive (but still costly) non-refundable ticket, there's no turning back. The charge will be immediately "imputed" to his charge account.

If sin is objective reality of the same unyielding character as the law of gravity or the rules of a big airline, then there must be a means of sustaining people until they come to the point of understanding sin and Christ's salvation. As we have seen, some never reach that point in this life because they die too young or have severe mental and emotional limitations. How, then, can people unable to respond to the Gospel be rescued?

Perhaps there is a clue in another, tragically true occurrence. A man in New York in a mean custody battle, jerked up his toddler-son, and leaped from a skyscraper. The innocent baby was subject to gravity as much as the father. The toddler did not make the choice to jump, but *shared the destiny* of the person who made that decision.

In Adam we all die because *he* made the decision to "jump" into sin, but in Christ we are all made alive because of *His* decision to follow righteousness. That's why Paul writes in Romans 5:10 that we are reconciled to the Father by His death on the cross, and saved by His life. However, as Paul says in Romans 6:23, salvation is a gift that must be freely received, otherwise there would be violation of our free will. To receive the gift of Jesus Christ and His salvation is to receive His destiny, not that of the "first" Adam.

Let's explore, then, some special cases to see how Christ's grace works.

The case of infants

An infant who dies is saved spiritually because it has never been separated from Jesus, His choices, and His destiny. The baby, even though born with a sin nature, is in the arms of Jesus and His grace until he or she reaches the point of understanding right and wrong, and makes a willful choice to select sin. That choice mounts up later in life to the rejection of grace. The person in that later stage cuts himself loose from Christ, on whom the "gravitational forces" of sin have no effect, and now begins his plunge toward judgment and Hell. Sin, at that point, is charged to his account.

Until that happens, the non-sinning (but sin-natured) baby is kept in Christ's grace. So David, under the illumination of the Holy Spirit declares of his deceased child: I will go to him, but he will not return to me." (2 Samuel 12:23) Little ones who die in their mother's womb or at any point prior to "actualizing" their sin nature by rejecting God righteousness and opting for sin go immediately to Heaven.

The case of the incapacitated

Those separated from knowledge of the Law because of physical, mental, or emotional incapacitation are still objectively guilty of sin. Yet those who once trusted Christ are still sustained by His grace when they are no longer able to make decisions aligning with His righteousness and will.

I think of a dear friend, a brilliant attorney, who stood tall for Christ. He and I fought hard spiritual battles side-by-side in the 1970s and early '80s. He never backed down from his passion for Christ and truth. Now, though, my old partner is in an advanced stage of Alzheimer's. I still see him when I travel to the city where he resides in a care facility. On the first encounter, I tried to recall old times with him, but he stared back blankly. Sometimes he looks angry, agitated, or in some other way out of character. The tree once sprouting a magnificent crop of the fruit of the Spirit is now just a ragged remnant, extending jagged branches. Yet my buddy still stands tall, upheld by the grace of the Jesus he served throughout his life. Death will be a wonderful release into rationality and quality of excellence even greater that of his best days on Earth.

Some of those incapacitated folk were *never* able to receive Christ. They are in the same state of the infant who does not understand sin and righteousness, right and wrong. The mentally and emotionally restricted are not animals—though sometimes treated as such—but are humans. That means on the one hand that they have a sin nature, but on the other hand because they cannot "actualize" it by willfully choosing sin, they are sustained by Christ's life and grace. When they die, they enter Heaven.

The case of suicide

On February 12, 2014, "popular and jovial" Pastor Allen "Tommy" Rucker took his gun behind the parsonage in Dunkerton, Iowa where he lived with his wife and shot himself.[39] "He was the epitome of a Christian," said Dick Ede, a member of the congregation. "He read the Bible constantly."

Pastor Isaac Hunter, founder and leader of the Summit Church in Orlando, killed himself after admitting to an affair. Not long before that the son of Pastor Rick Warren of California's Saddleback Church, took his own life. He had sat under his father's preaching and teaching, had heard the

---

[39] "'Godly' Iowa Pastor Who 'Read Bible Constantly' Takes Own Life Behind Church Parsonage," By Leonardo Blair, *The Christian Post,* February 13, 2014.

deep truths of "The Purpose-Driven Life," but was so clouded by depression he couldn't focus on the light.

Sometimes the darkness closes in so tightly even good people get separated from sanity. Pastor Ed Montgomery, co-founder with his wife, Jackie, of the Full Gospel Christian Assemblies International Church in Hazel Crest, Illinois, shows what leads to some suicides. A year after Jackie's death from a brain aneurysm he shot himself. "The Ed that I knew would never have wanted to leave his family," said Sandy Davis, Jackie's friend from childhood. Signs had already emerged that there might be a deeper problem. "He was saying he heard his wife's voice and footsteps and things like that," said Sandy Davis.

This is a good point to say something very important about the grieving process that I have learned after almost four decades of working with bereaved people: *Don't get stuck in one of the stages. Discipline yourself to keep moving forward.* Most of us who lose loved ones will fall into initial denial, then heat up in anger, then chill in despair. We must go through each one of these before we can come into acceptance and the great healing that comes with resolution. Being stuck in denial produces insanity. Remaining at the anger stage turns to bitterness. Being jammed in despair produces depression that can be deadly, as the case of Pastor Montgomery shows.

But he also demonstrates that there are times when some people are so separated from their true self and identity in Christ that they are once again like an infant in understanding, or a severely mentally disabled child, teen, or adult. A person who has confessed Christ, ministered Christ to others, manifested the fruit of the Spirit, and then takes his or own life is riding the parachute of grace through the void. The scope of that grace is captured by Paul in Romans 8:35-39:

> Who shall separate us from the love of Christ? Shall tribulation, or distress, or persecution, or famine, or nakedness, or peril, or sword? As it is written:
>
> "For Your sake we are killed all day long;
> We are accounted as sheep for the slaughter."
>
> Yet in all these things we are more than conquerors through Him who loved us. For I am persuaded that neither death nor life, nor angels nor principalities nor powers, nor things present nor things to come, nor height nor depth, nor any other created thing, shall be able to separate us from the love of God which is in Christ Jesus our Lord. (NKJV)

While suicide is not the unpardonable sin, neither should we excuse it. If you are now or have in the past contemplated taking your life, I wish you could go with me just one time to deal with a family bereaved through suicide and you will run from any thought of it, no matter how dark your world. Walk with me into the home where a young boy found his dead father in a bedroom closet, and try to help that child hold on to his own sanity as I had to do awhile back. Sit with me in the parlor of our church and join me in agonizing with a 13-year old girl who had to deal with her dad's suicide at just the point in her life when his acceptance and pride in her was essential to her identity and self-esteem.

A few experiences like that will make you realize how selfishly repugnant suicide is and the immensity of pain it brings to those left behind. And yet because of the big parachute of grace there is even hope of seeing loved ones in Heaven who truly knew Christ, but in desperation ended their own lives in this world.

3. God is going to reveal Himself to everyone whose heart is truly His… all who want to know Him.

We humans look at and pass judgment on people based on the outward appearance, but God views the heart. (1 Samuel 16:7) God looks on the heart of the infant in the womb, the mentally-emotionally-physically impaired individual in the wheelchair or moving about in mindless wandering, even the addled mind of the man or woman struggling in the claws of a maddening addiction.

Stephen Crane may not have intended it, but he captured the essence of God's compassionate understanding of those who cannot form words to speak to him. In a poem, Crane wrote,

> There was a man with tongue of wood
> Who essayed to sing,

> And in truth it was lamentable.
> But there was one who heard
> The clip-clapper of this tongue of wood
> And knew what the man Wished to sing,
> And with that the singer was content.

I have stood many times at the bedside of a person muted through disease and watched as they struggled to express their last thoughts. But God really knows the deepest issues surging in the heart of the person with "tongue of wood."

This I know, based on God's immutable word and loving character: *No human being whose heart longs to know God will miss Him!* None of us knows what transactions take place when all seems dark, even in "the valley of the shadow of death." Somehow, God is going to get His Gospel to people trapped in a condition that renders communication and even thought impossible.

Phillips Brooks was regarded by many as the greatest preacher in America in the latter half of the 19th century. His Boston pulpit was a monument to the power of preaching that hewed close to God's Word. Brooks was also a hymn writer. One especially rings true with what we have been considering here:

> How silently, how silently,
> The wondrous gift is giv'n
> So God imparts to human hearts
> The blessings of His heav'n.
> No ear may hear His coming,

> But in this world of sin,
> Where meek souls will receive Him,
> Still
> The dead Christ enters in.

Some think Brooks may have had a special friend in mind when he penned those words.

Down in Tuscumbia, Alabama, a young woman lived in profound isolation. Helen Keller was both blind and deaf. Without sight and hearing, she lived as if at the bottom of a great silent sea. Anne Sullivan, the godly woman who was Helen's teacher, was determined to lift up the girl into the joys of understanding and communication. Above all else, Anne Sullivan wanted Helen to know about God, and the salvation secured for her by the Lord Jesus Christ. Anne figured if anyone could help Helen understand it would by Phillips Brooks.

At last he had the opportunity to tell Helen the whole wonderful story of the Gospel. As he spoke, Anne Sullivan tapped out the words in the palm of Helen's hand, using the special code by which they communicated. As the message of Christ sunk in, Helen suddenly smiled. "Mr. Brooks," she said, "I have always known about God, but up until now I didn't know His name."

In her silent sightless world, God had found a receptive heart and Helen Keller had met Him in the deep where she lived. No one can come to Christ without the Holy Spirit's call, and Helen Keller shows that call can come in silence as well as thundering decibels.

One of the people I sought to help over many years was intensely addicted to alcohol. In more than 20 years of knowing him I cannot remember more than a half dozen coherent conversations. He was one of those alcoholics who found a way to stay drunk almost all the time. Yet toward the end of his life he brought me a document he had written. There was a surprising and great passion for Christ, a prophet's burden to warn people away from the kind of life he had lived, and an evangelist's zeal to bring people to Christ. I read his words and realized I had written him off too soon. I expect to see him in Heaven, and have wonderful, clear conversations with my beloved friend.

God is not willing that any should perish, but that all would come to the place of repentance. (2 Peter 3:9) That includes that baby you might have lost early in its life, or that incapacitated person over whom you shed so many tears, or even that confused, torn human being who ended his or her own earthly life in a moment of sheer insanity.

Don't give up hope of seeing them along with all the others on your first step in Heaven.

Chapter 10

ON YOUR FIRST STEP IN HEAVEN YOU WILL ENTER YOUR SPECIAL PLACE

On your first step in Heaven you will understand how special you are to the Father—and always have been.

The problem now is that the world and our own fragmented psyches block the full impact of this awareness. In our present existence, you and I "are not in the state of (our) creation," writes Blaise Pascal, the great 17th century mathematician and Christian philosopher. We struggle because we have "so little knowledge of what God is" that we do not "know" what we ourselves are, Pascal says, in his *Pensees*.

One of the chief things we do not know is how special we are to our Father. To borrow from a book title by Robert McGee, we "search for significance." We do so because we have lost our consciousness of our special stature in the special place God desires we occupy.

Irene and I have two children and six grandchildren. All of them have stayed with us during job changes, relocations, and other passages in their life-journeys. She and I talk about downsizing, but keep our present home—

which is too big for just the two of us—because we always want to be ready with a special place for them.

If that's the way I think as a fallen human dad, think of how much more God the Father values there being a "special place" for you and me as His own children. "If you then, being evil, know how to give good gifts to your children, how much more will your heavenly Father give the Holy Spirit to those who ask Him!" said Jesus. (Luke 11:13 NKJV) Your Abba keeps the biggest of "houses" because He has many children.

In the climactic days of His mission on earth, Jesus tells the men He soon will physically leave:

> "Do not let your heart be troubled; believe in God, believe also in Me. In My Father's house are many dwelling places; if it were not so, I would have told you; for I go to prepare a place for you. If I go and prepare a place for you, I will come again and receive you to Myself, that where I am, there you may be also." (John 14:1-3)

In the previous chapters, we have seen that on our first step in Heaven we put on a new body, perfectly fit for heavenly living. We immediately think, emotionally sense, and make choices through a new soul. We know those around us, including our loved ones from earth who entered Heaven before us, with a comprehension that beholds all their beauty as heavenly beings. We even see and know those that, back on earth, we thought were lost to us—our babies who died in the womb, or just after birth, or as toddlers, as well as older incapacitated loved ones who couldn't understand or respond to the Gospel, and even those who truly knew Christ, yet in a moment of profound darkness, took their own lives.

Now, as we dig deeply into the words of Jesus in John 14, we see just how special we are to our Father. When Jesus tells his original disciples He is going to prepare a place for them, He is speaking of all who will follow Him throughout history. That includes you and me.

First, then, let's look at how special you and I are to the Father *right now,* and why this is so. Centuries ago, through the Holy Spirit, King David got a flash of insight into the amazing attentiveness of the Father to His children. He exclaims:

> How precious also are Your thoughts to me, O God!
> How vast is the sum of them!
> If I should count them, they would outnumber the sand...
> (Psalm 139:17-18)

I have been a father for some 50 years, and there is never a moment when my daughter and son are not in my thoughts. I have been a grandfather for 25 years, and my thoughts continually default to them also. And what is the content of those thoughts? I desire constantly that they would be motivated and energized by passion for Christ and His Kingdom, that they would have the Holy Spirit's peace, and the Father's provision for health and prosperity, and His protection.

This is the prayer I have prayed for each of them every morning for years—so much that at times I fear it has become "vain repetition." Yet every time I consider changing the words I hear in my spirit, "keep on asking... keep on seeking... keep on knocking..." (Matthew 7:7) Again, as an earthly, fleshly Father, I am at least a fractional example of the immensity of God the Father's love and passion for you and me. If that's the way I think about my children and grandchildren, how "much more" our Father in Heaven thinks about us.

Why is this so? Why does the Father regard us as so special to His heart? Why are His thoughts focused on us constantly? How is it possible for Him to think of us all at once, and yet at the same time focus His mind on us as if we were His only child in the whole cosmos? If it is this way in our earthly lives, how can it be even greater in Heaven? How do His knowledge and thoughts about us determine the design of the "place" He has prepared for us in Heaven?

The reason why

The reason God the Father's thoughts are on us constantly in a special way is because through Christ we are His *covenant* children. That means we are His "blood kin." The word "covenant" in Old Testament Hebrew is *berit,* and in the Greek of the New Testament, *diatheke.* Our English term, "covenant", refers to "coming together" in an intimate bond. In Hebrew, especially, it also carries the concept of "cutting" because covenant-partners would often formalize the bond between them by sacrificing an animal, cutting the body in two, walking between the halves. Covenant-makers would also usually cut their own hands and exchange blood to symbolize the seriousness of commitment to one another.

Our hope of salvation emerges first in Genesis 3:15, when God tells the devil-serpent that He would bring from the seed of the woman a descendant who will crush the deadly enemy's head. As God establishes covenant with Abraham, accompanied by shedding of blood, the Lord reveals that Abraham's progeny will bring forth that Savior, who would also be foreseen in prophetic revelation across history.

All who freely receive the salvation Jesus Christ achieves for humanity become the covenant children of God. The whole of humanity can call Him "Father" in the sense that He "sired" or created them, but only covenant children can call God the Father *Abba*—"Daddy."

Many years ago I had a friend named Jimmy Wells. In those early high school years I was already fascinated by media, especially television, which was in its infancy. I began hanging out at a local TV station, which in those dawning years didn't have videotape to rely on for programming, so all the local productions had to be live. At times the producers let me function as an assistant to the floor manager. Jimmy Wells' father was a camera operator. As such he became something of a hero to me, someone I aspired to be like.

One day he took Jimmy and me to a company picnic. Someone asked him if Jimmy and I were his sons. I still remember how I, as a boy growing up without a father, winced at the only words that in fairness to Mr. Wells he could utter: "He is my son (pointing to Jimmy), but he's (pointing to me) not." Mr. Wells was simply saying that Jimmy was the son springing from the covenant between himself and his wife, a relationship I did not share.

The realization of the exclusion was for a brief moment devastating. And yet I knew Mr. Wells had made provision for my lunch that day, and that he would hasten to protect me as much as Jimmy if danger loomed. I even knew that if I needed shelter, and my mother gave permission, Mr. Wells would take me under his own roof.

Mr. Wells had affection for me, but I was not in the role of Jimmy, his "covenant-son." By the way, whenever a husband and wife adopt a child, that little one also becomes a covenant child even though they may not share their parents' blood. Adoption brings a child into covenant as if he or she had been physically sired by the man they recognized as "Dad" and emerged from the womb of the woman they called "Mom".

That's how we became the covenant children of God. "For you have not received a spirit of slavery leading to fear again, but you have received a spirit of adoption as sons (and daughters) by which we cry out, "Abba"! "Father"! writes Paul, in Romans 8:15.

This places us "in" God's only begotten Son, and we become heirs with Him of everything God the Father has promised to God the Son. We receive the inner witness of the Spirit Who "testifies with our spirit that we are children of God," and if we are God's children in the same sense as His only begotten Son, we are "heirs also, heirs of God and fellow heirs with Christ." (Romans 8:16-17)

Therefore, we are as special to God the Father, our Abba, to the same degree as Jesus Christ is special to the Father!

"See what an incredible quality of love the Father has given shown, bestowed on us, that we should be permitted to be named and called and counted the children of God! And so we are! The reason that the world does not know recognize, acknowledge us is that it does not know recognize, acknowledge Him." (1 John 3:1 AMP)

This exclusivity is so great we can have it only in the context of community. Without brothers and sisters sin makes us selfish spoiled brats. And yet in a healthy family all the siblings feel themselves special in daddy's eyes, and the family of God is the healthiest of all!

Our Father is not bound by the sequence of kronos-time. He doesn't have to try to schedule time for this child or that. He is present in our time, but not bound by it. God's transcendence means He can be immanent in all moments with all His covenant children as if they were His only child. Yet for the sake of our mental and emotional well-being and cultivation of our nature as relational beings in His image, He places us in the "fellowship of the saints," a big family that spans time. A measure, in fact, of our true relationship to the Father is in loving our brothers and sisters—even if, as is true in almost all families in the fallen world—we don't always like them!

'Custom-made'

Second, consider how the place prepared for you is a place *specially* prepared for you. To grasp the beauty of what Jesus is saying here about the place prepared for us we must once again look at the human scale, and see how it reflects in its limited, blurred way the heavenly scale.

In the ancient Middle East, and continuing today in many cultures, a measure of success was in providing a family compound for your loved ones. Children and grandchildren would have their own homes and lives within the compound. The loving patriarch would have as one of his life goals that of building that special community if it did not already exist. Lot, for example, was the nephew of Abraham, and lived with his own family within the compound until he chose to leave it. Job's immense sorrow was over the destruction of his sons and daughters, not only individually, but as the unit within the compound. His great joy was in the coming of new sons and daughters and the creation of a new compound.

Tribes across history have found this the best way of living. Political theorists try to use tribalism to argue that socialism is the foundational way of community living. They miss the point that the sharing of property was not coerced but freely entered into between the family members within the compound. This is the picture Jesus is presenting in John

14. God the Father is the "Family Patriarch." Heaven is the "Family Compound" where His children live in their own "dwelling places" centered around His Throne of glory.

Once I dreamt of having a family compound. Irene and I bought a small Texas ranch, and built what we thought would be our retirement home there. I walked the land, and envisioned the sections I would offer to our daughter and son, so they could build homes. We would all dwell together blissfully inside the compound.

As I contemplated the homes they might build, I thought of what they might look like. I would not make of our little community a "neighborhood association" with all kinds of rules to enforce conformity. If our daughter wanted a home painted in bright colors, she would have it. If our son wanted to construct a rustic log-house, he would be free to do so. I wanted the dwelling places within the compound to be according to their styles and tastes.

There would be general guidelines for the Henley family compound: Whatever built there would have to be endurable, and done with quality—no shacks for mere overnighting, no tent cities, or anything else conflicting with the esthetic values Irene and I hold dear and that we have tried to nurture in our family. Yet we would have wanted them to build according to their tastes.

Again, as a father I am a faint shadow of the heart and mind of God the Father. That means He wants your dwelling place within the Family Compound of Heaven to be in accord with the preferences that align with His character, given uniquely to you.

When we are at our best we are simply following the choices and inclinations God has created within us. Paul writes that "it is God who is at work in you, both to will and to work for His good pleasure." (Philippians 2:13) Remember the first time we encountered the pleasure of God? It was way back in Genesis. Our Creator surveyed all He had made, "and behold, it was very good." (Genesis 1:31) This is the artist standing back at the finished canvas and sighing with satisfaction, or the sculptor looking at the completed work with enjoyment, or the contractor taking aerial photos of an architectural masterpiece he has built and feeling immense pleasure.

So the Father wants you to know such joy in your dwelling place in Heaven's Family Compound. If in building our imaginary Henley compound my children start by recognizing, appreciating and respecting first of all the character Irene and I possess, they would be able to build whatever they desire. "Delight yourself in the Lord and He will give you the desires of your heart," says Psalm 137:4. This is because the more your delight is in God and His ways the more your desires are like His.

And yet, as noted, Heaven's Family Compound is not a neighborhood association, enforcing conformity. Some reading this book delight in Nordic minimalism, while others want delicate French provincialism, and still others gothic seriousness, Victorian dressiness, ranch-style casual, New England quaint, or hunting lodge rustic.

How is your "style" addressed in Heaven?

In 1971 I made a trip literally around the world, from Baltimore back to our home at that time near Washington, DC. After almost a month of travel, I was ready—and had been for a couple of weeks—to go home. There was the thrill of stepping off the airplane at Washington's Reagan Airport, and rushing into the arms of Irene and our children. And when we got to our home out in the Virginia suburbs, I entered a "dwelling place" prepared just for me. Welcome home banners, my favorite meal, and a pristine-clean home were all there.

Why? Because Irene knew me and my preferences, and what I would hope to encounter when I arrived home. I was special to her as she is to me, and she worked hard to get it just right!

You are special to God the Father, and He knows you intimately, and therefore the house Jesus builds for you will be in accord with your "tastes" and "desires." But what do those words mean in this context? Color of paint? Style of design? Type of construction materials? No, it's much deeper than that.

When I got home from my globe-circling journey I could have walked into an architectural style that I detested and décors I loathed, and still been completely happy. The reason: it was the quality, not the quantitative appearance. The "tastes" by which Jesus prepares our dwelling place in Heaven's Family Compound are in accord with the personality God has given us in our earthly self.

Your essential personality continues in your heavenly self because personality is shaped by our spiritual gifts. God gave you special capacities for your mission in the world, and designed your personality even before you were made to be the vessel that carried and expressed your gifts in service for Christ and His Kingdom. Thus you will in Heaven be the *real you*, the *best you* because all the constrictions and blemishes with which sin mars our souls have been removed.

The prophet Jeremiah is an example of the continuation of our essential personality, shaped by our callings and gifts. "Before I formed you in the womb I knew you... before you were born I consecrated you; I have appointed you a prophet to the nations," God told him. (Jeremiah 1:5) Jeremiah's calling was to be a prophet, and so he received prophetic gifting and anointing (empowerment). All this was done in pre-earth time and therefore it is eternal in scope. The prophetic personality is distinct. In the flesh, prophets can be grumpy and hard to live with. Under the Holy Spirit, brute honesty becomes a personality whose truthfulness is something others can rely on. Rather than crabbiness the Spirit-led (as opposed to flesh-directed) prophet tells truth in a way that inspires others to walk the right path.

Jeremiah's personality is going to desire straight lines, things that aren't too fussy. Your gift may be exhortation or encouragement, so your personality may delight in bright colors and sweeping lines. Perhaps you have a shepherd gifting, or that of hospitality. Your personality needs roominess so you can entertain people and care for them.

Since no one will be needy in Heaven, you will enjoy space to fellowship with others, and relish their pleasure.

The Lord knows you and He knows the real you. The place Jesus prepares for you in Heaven is custom-made. When He says, "I am going to prepare a place for you" He doesn't mean any old place. The context of His words is found in passages like Exodus 23:20, where God tells Moses regarding His covenant child, Israel, "I am going to send an angel before you to guard you along the way and to bring you into the place which I have prepared." (Exodus 23:20)

The Holy Spirit preserves the memory of this through the Psalmist, who writes, in Psalm 78:53-53,

> He led forth His own people like sheep
> And guided them in the wilderness like a flock;
> He led them safely, so that they did not fear;
> But the sea engulfed their enemies.

Since, as Paul writes in 1 Corinthians 10:11 everything that happened to the Old Testament covenant children is an example of our walk as God's covenant children, then the very angels of God are guarding us as we move toward the prepared place. But like Thomas we don't know where the "prepared place" is, so how do we know the way? Numbers 10:33 describes how at the crucial point in Israel's passage toward the Promised Land that the Ark of the Covenant went before them to search out and prepare a resting place. The Ark was the place where God manifested His presence to the Hebrew wanderers. The cloud that guided the covenant people through the wilderness rested above it, and marked the route to the prepared place. So, two great truths emerge from these images.

First, from the day you enter covenant relationship with the Lord His angels begin guiding your journey all the way home, to your specially prepared place. Second, you are not going to get lost along the way if you truly trust Him, because His presence goes before you. He guides you through the "wilderness" of this world. And in the final stage of the journey you don't cross through the valley of the shadow in desperate solitude, but He is with you and before you, and goes ahead of you to prepare the place for you.

Thumbs up!

Through the years I have had opportunity to work with refugees from lands where they had suffered unimaginable cruelty and persecution. Once, changing planes in Tokyo, I saw a long line of Cambodians waiting to board a plane to the United States. They were fleeing the "killing fields" of the satanic Pol Pot regime in their native country. A teenaged boy toward the end of the line fixed his eyes on me, an American. They were full of hope and anticipation, and he smiled and gave me a thumbs-up. He was on his way to the home that was being prepared for him by the humanitarian agencies or individuals sponsoring him and his family. I wept as I saw the joy in his face and sensed the excitement in his heart.

But some of the most haunting words I have ever heard came from the mouth of a weary refugee woman from one the world's cruelest nations. She had become a follower of Christ in her native land, and been thrown into prison. The guards respected neither her age nor gender, and treated her so severely they broke her shoulder. Miraculously, she got out of prison, and was able to join relatives here in America, in Houston. Eventually she wound up at our church, and some of our leaders helped her get asylum.

One day I could tell she was very sad. "What's the matter?" I asked. She searched for words in English, the language so new to her. She didn't know how to make her answer subtle, nuanced, or dressed-up. All she could speak was the ache in her heart. Here's what she said: *"I miss me."*

She didn't mean that in the sense of some pampered egotist, or self-worshipping *prima donna*. She was saying that the "me" she missed in her exile from her homeland was the person she was there—the daughter, wife, mother, professional person. All that had made her life special and made the place special for her. Every time I bumped into her in the halls of our church she would bow in the attempt to thank me, as a representative of the congregational leadership that had literally saved her life. But she yearned for home where she had once lived in what she considered the essence of her being.

There is a sense in which we all miss "me." But it's not the "me" of this sin-shadowed world. It's the "me" created and designed uniquely by the Father whose manifest presence we have lost because of sin, and who Himself is the "special place" for which we were made and which was made just for us. Home is where we can relax and be "ourselves." If this is true in an earthly sense, imagine how much more in our "dwelling place" in Heaven, where we at last have the freedom of being our true selves!

You and I are on assignment in this world. We are like the ex-pats of a large global corporation, sent to a foreign land to get a job done. We are in this world to contribute to the advance of God's Kingdom of righteousness, peace, and joy in the Holy Spirit. (Romans 14:17; see also Matthew 24:14) We are thankful for the gift of life on earth, but we know we are not home. The more we walk with Christ, the more we recognize the world is the place of our mission, but not our true home. When our assignment here is over, we get to go home! (Psalm 139:16)

In our early years, Irene and I and our children moved a lot. She has always had a special gifting for making all the houses "home." She always told us, "Home is wherever we are together." Home is with God, our Abba-Father. In Christ, He Himself has gone out before us, to prepare a perfect place for us, one suited to the real "me," the real you, because He knows us intimately through the Holy Spirit.

I spoke earlier of the little ranch and home we had built there for our retirement. Almost a decade into that experience, we began to realize that it was not our stopping place after all, so we sold it. In a much greater sense, this world is not our stopping place. If we regard it as that we will become raw existentialists, living only for the moment and the best we can squeeze from our lives here on earth. In fact the Greek word in John 14 for the Father's *house* conveys the idea of the place one returns to at the end of the journeying of an entire lifetime.

So "sell the house" of this world. Don't put all your hope here on earth. Follow the Ark of His manifest presence, and know Jesus, who doesn't merely tell you the way, but who *is* the way. He will take you to your real home, specially prepared for the special person you are to your Father, your Abba, and always have been.

www.ingramcontent.com/pod-product-compliance
Lightning Source LLC
Chambersburg PA
CBHW071921290426
44110CB00013B/1432